Pelican Books
Growing Out of Crime

Hugh Campbell

May 1986

Andrew Rutherford

Growing Out of Crime

Penguin Books

Penguin Books Ltd, Harmondsworth, Middlesex, England
Viking Penguin Inc., 40 West 23rd Street, New York, New York 10010, U.S.A.
Penguin Books Australia Ltd, Ringwood, Victoria, Australia
Penguin Books Canada Limited, 2801 John Street, Markham, Ontario, Canada L3R 1B4
Penguin Books (N.Z.) Ltd, 182–190 Wairau Road, Auckland 10, New Zealand

First published 1986

Typeset, printed and bound in Great Britain by
Hazell Watson & Viney Ltd
Member of the BPCC Group,
Aylesbury, Bucks
Filmset 10/13pt VIP Palatino

For Tim, Annabel and Max

Contents

Preface

If a young person becomes involved in crime or other trouble-some behaviour, it is tempting for parents or teachers to imagine that the responsibility and solution lie elsewhere. By creating a network of criminal justice, welfare and mental health arrangements, public policy holds out the seductive offer of an institutional fix; although the offer may be appealing, it is not an answer. If young people are to grow out of troublesome behaviour, the home, school and other developmental institutions must be encouraged and equipped to hold on during difficult and sometimes volatile phases. Formal intervention carries the threat of exile from a normal environment, and the consequently inevitable waste of a chance for normal growth and development. Existing policy trends must be reversed so as to direct attention to the everyday and intuitive practice which holds the most promise.

This book is intended mainly for persons directly coping with young people who are involved in crime or other troubling behaviour. I hope that parents, teachers, youth workers, social workers, probation officers and magistrates may all be encouraged to hold on to such children and to shun inducements to let them go.

Many people have made this book possible. I am especially indebted to Chris Green, Pauline Owen, and the staff and young people associated with the Woodlands Centre; Richard Kay of the Rainer Foundation (who once said that he and I, both once borstal assistant-governors, had been 'born again'); David Harding of the BBC, with whom I worked on two radio

9

programmes, *The Massachusetts Alternative* and *The Child Fixers*, which contributed to Chapters Three and Five, and Gerry Northam of the BBC who reported *The Child Fixers*; the Hilden Charitable Fund; Ira Schwartz of the Hubert H. Humphrey Institute of Public Affairs at the University of Minnesota; Colleagues on NACRO's juvenile crime advisory committee; Edward Murphy and colleagues in the Massachusetts Department of Youth Services; Lloyd Ohlin, recently of the Harvard Law School; Jerry Miller of the National Center for Institutions and Alternatives; and the staff and young people with whom I worked in three borstals.

My appreciation is also due to: Diana Marshallsay and Joan Hoyle of the University of Southampton Library; Christine Hardwick for preparation of the index; Margaret Newton, who, with care and cheer, typed the manuscripts through several drafts; Julian Rutherford; Timothy and Annabel Rutherford, who helped me to hold on to the manuscript; and, finally, to Judith Rutherford, whose efficient editing and support is reflected throughout the book.

Chapter One

A Chance to Mature

What the child can do for us later – or that it is cheaper to be good to children now – should not be our primary concern. Children should claim our attention because they engage our humanitarian feelings. A child must be loved and supported for what the child is now, not just for what the child can become . . . children are fellow humans and claim an equal place with other age groups because they are human beings, not because they give some future return on investment. (Orville G. Brim and Jerome Kagan, 1980, p. 22)

Crime is not a 'thing'. Crime is a concept applicable in certain social situations where it is possible and in the interests of one or several parties to apply it. We can create crime by creating systems that ask for the word. We can extinguish crime by creating the opposite kinds of systems. (Nils Christie, 1982, p. 74)

It seems incredible that regimes which seem to involve large numbers of staff for case conferences on boys' welfare cannot, on the other hand, offer sufficient night supervision for boys to go to the lavatory in a civilized way .. efforts to prevent the development of prison language among the boys seem rather pointless at the sight of a number of children, each clasping a potty, drifting to the latrines in the mornings. (Spencer Millham, Roger Bullock and Kenneth Hosie, 1978, p. 117)

•

Despite common-sense objections that exile and incarceration only make matters worse, shades of the prison house are closing in on increasing numbers of young people. In 1973 some 17,000 persons aged between fourteen and twenty were

11

sentenced to prison system institutions. Ten years later this number had almost doubled, having increased to 30,000. It has been among persons of under seventeen years that the increase has been sharpest, and the proportion of such cases dealt with by the courts has risen threefold in the twenty-five years up to 1985. The trend has little to do with violent crime and largely reflects more severe sentencing of young people convicted of property offences.

During the 1980s the population of young people will decline by 20 per cent. Although school closures are widespread, the logic of demographics does not extend to the prison system. Two thousand additional cells for young people are included in the prison system's construction programme announced at the start of the decade. This investment in the apparatus of imprisonment is directly counter to the view that, with support and encouragement, most young people mature out of crime. These conditions are found not in prison cells and corridors, but in the settings where most young people grow up.

The most effective resources for coping with and resolving the problems of young people and crime are located in the home and school. The great majority of events involving young people which might have been called criminal are not brought to the attention of police because they are absorbed by home, school or other developmental institutions, such as places of work, recreation and worship. The troubles get worse when the matter is removed from the home and school to the institutional arrangements of criminal justice, welfare or mental health. This book is a preliminary exploration of what happens when priority is given to developmental institutions in managing young people and crime.

The traditional approaches to young people and crime are, in convenient shorthand, punishment, welfare and treatment. Each approach continues to enjoy fashionable seasons, often

12

with excesses in one direction prompting a resurgence by one of the other approaches. All that is new is the language which, for a while, might obscure exactly which approach is in vogue at the time. The assumptions are that young people involved in crime and other troublesome events represent, respectively, depravity, social deprivation and personal pathology. Despite their differences each of the traditional approaches, ultimately, leads to exile from home and school and placement in an incarcerative institution. By contrast, the developmental approach regards crime and other misbehaviour by young people as a transient and integral part of the process of growing up. Instead of exclusion, the approach seeks absorption and fortifies the developmental role of home and school. If there is to be a self-fulfilling prophecy, it is that sooner rather than later matters will be worked out. As with other childish things, misbehaviour eventually will be put away.

The developmental approach has remained largely unarticulated, because it is rarely considered in policy terms. The intuitive quality of the approach finds its most powerful expression within the home when the child in trouble is one's own; the protective and supportive instincts of the family have not yet been used for policy purposes. However, if policy is to be addressed to seeing young people through troubled phases, steps must be taken to begin to build upon intuitive responses. The four basic propositions underscoring the developmental approach are:

- The principal sources of support and control for young people are in the home and the school.
- When formal intervention is invoked this should, to the greatest possible extent, be focused primarily on enhancing the strengths of home and school.
- Only in the most exceptional cases should formal intervention separate a young person from developmental

13

institutions, and any period of separation should be kept to the minimum required for other purposes.

- Formal interventions, especially when using incarceration, are disruptive in two crucial senses. First, the normal growth and development of the young person is threatened. Second, the capacity for developmental institutions to be effective is weakened.

The developmental approach does not mean ignoring or taking no action on youth crime. Far from being passive, the approach insists that intervention be primarily the responsibility of those institutions with a commitment to the young person. In this sense the developmental approach has a rather different emphasis from Edwin Schur's notion of 'radical non-intervention'. Schur argued, in the early 1970s, that what young people involved in crime

suffer from, more than either problems of the psyche or socio-economic distress, is contingencies. Processing contingencies significantly shape delinquency rates and, in large measure, also determine which specific individuals reach the various stages in the juvenile justice process ... the basic injunction for public policy becomes *leave kids alone wherever possible*. This effort partly involves mechanisms to divert children away from the courts but it goes further to include opposing various kinds of intervention by diverse social control and socializing agencies. (Schur, 1973, pp. 154–5)

The more positive emphasis implied by the developmental approach seeks to strengthen intervention by homes and schools to enable these institutions to deal directly with the problem, to hold on to young people and, thereby, to avoid or limit formal intervention.

The distinctive features of the developmental approach can be sketched out further by a comparison with the three traditional approaches. The punishment approach is considered first, as it remains the predominant one, even though it is often camouflaged by fashionable jargon.

The principal elements of the punishment approach are:

- Most crime is a matter of opportunity and rational choice.
- In so far as a person is responsible for his/her actions, he/she should be held accountable.
- The sole justification for punishment should be commission of a specifically defined offence.
- Punishment is a valid response to criminal behaviour as an expression of society's disapproval and as an individual and general deterrent.
- There should be proportionality between the seriousness of the crime and the penalty.

Overlapping elements are found in any consideration of the welfare and treatment approaches. These approaches are often merged, and the two terms can in some cases be used interchangeably.*

The principal elements of the welfare approach are:

- Delinquent, dependent and neglected young people are all products of an adverse environment which, at its worst, is characterized by multiple deprivation.
- All young people in trouble can be effectively dealt with through a single uniform process designed to identify and meet their needs.
- Prevention of neglect and alleviation of disadvantage will lead to the prevention of crime.

Finally, the principal elements of the treatment approach are:

- Crime is a pathological condition and is symptomatic of some deeper maladjustment.
- The underlying disorder of which crime is symptomatic is susceptible to diagnosis and treatment.
- Given the wide variation in young people's needs, flexi-

* See, for example, the Black Report (1979, pp. 32–4), from which many of the elements set out here are taken.

bility and wide discretion are essential to determine the appropriate treatment.

- Effective treatment technologies are available, and the informed consent by the recipient can be obtained.

Whereas the punishment approach stresses formality of procedures, both the welfare and the treatment approaches encourage informality as the principal way of identifying and meeting individual needs. As Nils Christie has reminded us, punishment has to do with the delivery of pain and for this reason, especially when applied to young persons, it is disguised by more palatable language. Note, for example, the ambivalence of a House of Commons Select Committee:

> While it would be regrettable if there were any general identification of residential care with punishment, it is a fact of life that one category of children in care for whom residential care may be essential are those children whose behaviour is leading them further and further down the path of anti-social behaviour. (Select Committee on Social Services, 1984, p. lxxxii)

A government research report has commented upon the prevalence of linguistic acrobatics: 'In all the jargon about security and treatment, it seemed very easy for the referring agencies to forget they were asking for people to be locked up' (Cawson and Martell, 1979, p. 209).

Punishment continues to be the dominant approach. This has been the case since the reaction during the late eighteenth century to arbitrary and capricious vengeance. Cesare Beccaria's essay 'Dei deilitti e delle pene' of 1766 gave momentum to criminal law reform in Europe and beyond; Beccaria's reappearance two centuries later was largely a reaction to the excesses committed in the name of treatment and welfare. Incarcerating young people for periods which far outweighed the seriousness of their offences or subjecting them to intrusive forms of therapy prompted liberals to talk of the young person's 'right to punishment' (Fox, 1974). Under the banners of 'justice model' or 'just deserts' the notion of proportionality between the harm done and the dosage of pain was restored as an ideal. Powerfully influential was a twenty-volume set of juvenile justice standards produced by the American Bar Association. The president of the National Council of Juvenile Court Judges commented in 1977:

All of a sudden it has been decided that the 'just desserts' [sic] rationale is the only answer to juvenile crime. This has never worked for the adult system and there is no reason to believe it will work with children. Critics of the juvenile justice system forget that the juvenile court was created to get children out of the 19th century 'just desserts' [sic] criminal justice system. (Driscoll, 1977)

The roots of the Welfare approach go back to efforts in the middle of the nineteenth century to rescue young people from prison or from their social circumstances. Yet the welfare approach inevitably leads back into incarcerative institutions. In the early 1980s, almost one third of the 90,000 children 'in care' in England and Wales were held in residential institutions. As one official research study concluded: 'It is rather frightening that the capacity for rejection in the child care system should seem to be so endless' (Cawson and Martell, 1979, p. 215). In 1984 the Select Committee on Social Services acknowledged the serious long-term emotional and developmental effects of growing up in residential institutions but went on to remark that 'there is nothing inherently wrong with some older children remaining for months or even years in residential care' (Select Committee on Social Services, 1984, p. lxxx).

The treatment approach sprang from efforts by early criminologists to locate causes of crime within the biological make-up or psyche of the individual. The emerging professions of psychiatry and social work were quick to recognize the opportunities. The treatment approach looks to incarcerative institutions to provide the required 'therapeutic

17

community' or the 'structured setting' for a backbone implant. Incarceration also is required for those young people who are not 'amenable' to treatment programmes in the community, and especially when this non-amenability is displayed by letting the programme down. Treatment's search for amenable clients inevitably widens the criminal justice net. Not surprisingly many treatment professionals gravitate towards so-called diversion and prevention programmes.

The three traditional approaches to young people in trouble should be considered in relation not only to the institutional arrangements of criminal justice, but also to those of welfare and mental health. The boundaries of these three types of institutional arrangement are far from rigid, suggesting to Paul Lerman of Rutgers University that there is 'a youth-in-trouble system', encompassing all three arenas. As Lerman notes, the underlying dynamic is often one of economics, exemplified by 'an increasing incentive to redefine youth in trouble according to diagnostic categories which will legitimate placement in facilities deemed appropriate for reimbursement' (Lerman, 1982, p. 150). The expansion of private mental health incarceration of young people in the United States is one striking example of the source of payment defining the nature of the young person's misbehaviour.

These considerations allow policy and practice to be viewed within a 'youth-in-trouble matrix'. As shown below, the matrix takes account of the three traditional approaches as well as the developmental approach, and the institutional arrangement primarily associated with each approach. Shown are the four types of approach, each of which, as indicated by 'P', is primarily associated with a particular institutional arrangement. With the exception of developmental institutions, institutional arrangements can also be expected to follow secondary approaches, as indicated by 'S'.

The matrix serves as a reminder that there is more than a

	Youth-in-trouble Matrix			
Approach	Institutional Arrangement			
	Criminal Justice	Welfare	Mental Health	Developmental
Punishment	P	S	S	
Welfare	S	P	S	
Treatment	S	S	P	
Developmental	S	S	S	P

single type of institutional arrangement. Although this book deals mostly with the threat to normal growth and development posed by criminal justice arrangements, nothing is gained by substituting one form of disruptive intervention for another. Welfare and mental health interventions also carry the potential of undermining developmental institutions. Policy which is conceived exclusively in criminal justice terms perpetuates the segmentation which has served to thwart the developmental approach.

For young people, the negative consequences of exposure to criminal justice have been amply demonstrated. Marvin Wolfgang, who directed a long-term study of youngsters growing up in Philadelphia, concluded: 'the juvenile justice system, at its best, has no effect on the subsequent behaviour of adolescent boys and, at its worst, has a deleterious effect on future behaviour' (Wolfgang et al., 1972, p. 252). In England, similar conclusions were reached on the basis of the Cambridge longitudinal study. David Farrington found that a first conviction is likely to lead to further offending (Farrington, 1977, p. 283). This point was extended by Donald West: '. . . processing delinquents through the juvenile justice system, especially if it involves any substantial period of detention within penal establishments, is more likely to

19

exacerbate than to reduce anti-social behaviour' (West, 1982, p. 143).

That incarcerative institutions are so lamentably unsuccessful with young people should not be surprising when account is taken of how they obstruct and retard essential areas of growth from child to adult. At this age preoccupying concerns might be to resolve 'uncertainty over sexual adequacy, interpersonal power, autonomy of belief and action, and acceptability to peers' (Kagan, 1979, p. 110). Where should this resolution take place? What should be the setting of Erik Erikson's 'quest for identity'? The potentially crippling impact of incarceration is even more apparent when viewed against the needs of young people moving towards adulthood: to learn effectively to manage their own affairs and make choices; to relate to persons differing in social class, age and sex, the latter being essential for psycho-sexual development; and to experience the sense of responsibility that comes from having other people dependent on one's actions. It would be difficult to design a method more certain than incarcerative institutions to thwart normal development. As the Royal College of Psychiatrists stated in 1984: 'Prolonged residential care is likely to lead to abnormal psychological development' (Select Committee on Social Services, 1984, vol. III, p. 599). The American sociologist John Irwin has written of 'state-raised' youths: 'The world view of these youths is distorted, stunted or incoherent. To a great extent, the youth prison is their only world, and they think almost entirely in the categories of this world' (Irwin, 1970, p. 29). Jack Henry Abbot, in correspondence with Norman Mailer, wrote: 'At age 37 I am barely a precocious child. My passions are those of a boy' (Abbott, 1982, p. 15).

In England and Wales a little over half of all known indictable offenders in 1983 were aged under twenty-one, and one third were under seventeen. For burglary, about seven out of ten were under twenty-one. These official data have many limitations. They refer only to offences which have resulted in a formal caution or finding of guilt; no account is taken of the events which have been handled in some other way, or which remain undetected. For example, only one burglary in five is cleared up. As young people are more likely than adults to offend in company, they are responsible for fewer offences than the number of known offenders suggests. Young people may be more easily detected and arrested than adults. Finally, formal cautioning is used to a much greater extent with juveniles than adults and, to the extent that formal cautions are not a substitute for guilt findings, the number of known offenders will be inflated.

From the published official crime statistics, Table 1 below sets out data on offenders of age and sex.

Table 1   Known (indictable) offenders per 1,000 in each age group by sex and age 1983

Age group	Males	Females
10–13	29	9
14–16	75	17
17–20	69	10
21+	13	2

(Abstracted from *Criminal Statistics 1983*, p. 103, Table 5.20)

Peaks and Lows

Both official statistics and self-report studies suggest that the peak ages for many offences are those from fifteen to seventeen, coinciding, it might be noted, with the peak of physical growth. But as David Farrington has concluded, there is an absence of basic information about the development of delinquent activity (Farrington, 1981, p. 29). Similarly, David

Greenberg, noting the relative absence of empirical research seeking or testing explanations for the contrasting peak ages of arrest, remarks that 'there can be no certainty as to the relative importance of the motivations, control considerations, and opportunities that give rise to the various involvement patterns for different offences' (Greenberg, 1983, p. 34).

Data presented for a single year can be misleading, as these do not permit age effects (patterns of variation in crime rates with age) to be distinguished from an influence on a given cohort of young people that persists as the cohort ages. Nor does it take account of the influence of a particular period that does not persist at a later time (Greenberg, 1983, pp. 31–2).

Longitudinal studies, especially when both official and self-report data are obtained, have filled some of the gaps in what is known about offending patterns by age. A major study conducted by the Cambridge Institute of Criminology found that shoplifting, stealing from vehicles and other theft tend to be most frequent at relatively early ages. For example, shoplifting peaks between the ages of fourteen and sixteen, whereas assault, damaging property and drug use tend to peak between seventeen and twenty. This general pattern is confirmed by self-report data. For most offences the peak age of incidence is within a year or two of the seventeenth birthday, with assault and drug use declining with age less quickly than other offences.

The Cambridge study differentiated between 'temporary recidivists' (juvenile recidivists with no convictions between nineteen and twenty-four) and 'persisting recidivists'. The two groups differed across a wide range of life-style attributes, with most temporary recidivists found to be similar to persons without criminal records. West summarized the main findings:

Every comparison we could make showed that the persisting

recidivists were a disfavoured and deviant group, whereas the temporary recidivists were much closer to and often indistinguishable from the non-delinquents . . . at age twenty-four, persisting recidivists continued to be significantly socially deviant, whereas men whose conviction careers had definitely ended had become as conformist in lifestyle as men who never had a criminal record. (West, 1982, pp. 79–81)

The shift to normality by the temporary recidivists was slow, and explanatory factors remain unexplored. In this respect the only distinguishing feature was the tendency to cease going about in large groups. Similarly, an American study directed by Jackson Toby suggested that integration with close female friends and family members predicts adult adjustment, and that continued involvement with male friends and peer group gangs presages additional criminal behaviour in adulthood (cited in Cline, 1980, p. 662).

Marvin Wolfgang coined the term 'spontaneous remission' to describe young people's desistance from crime. Similarly, Donald West concluded: 'The behaviour of delinquents genuinely and spontaneously changes in the direction of increasing social conformity with increasing age' (West, 1982, p. 252). The developmental rationale appears to have had an important effect on public policy in the Netherlands. An official at the Ministry of Justice has written:

The realization, that in general this behaviour constitutes but a phase in a youngster's life as well as the fact that the juvenile justice system handles only a minor selection of all misbehaving juveniles, has made authorities far more tolerant of both problem behaviour and delinquency. It has also made the police, prosecutors and juvenile judges far more reluctant to interfere in the lives of children. (Junger-Tas, p. 3)

The policy implications of the developmental approach have also been explored by the American legal scholar Frank Zimring, who refers to 'the social value of giving young offenders a chance to mature'. The policy is 'to enhance the opportunity to survive adolescence without a major sacrifice in life chances'. Zimring explicitly notes that the policy does not necessarily rule out punishment, but is one that 'facilitates growth, avoids permanent stigma, the isolation of young offenders from community settings, or any other form of exile from the larger society in which they are expected to grow'. Zimring makes the important point that 'values may indicate policies designed to achieve these ends even if a substantial minority of the young do not outgrow patterns of law violation . . . reform is a process in which time, the offender's efforts, and the resources in the community at large play their parts; the use of coercive state power may sometimes unduly disrupt the process' (Zimring, 1978, pp. 79–80). The principle that young people have the chance to mature reflects the central theme of this book.

The developmental approach is explored in subsequent chapters. Chapter Two examines missed opportunities to fashion new approaches to young people in trouble in Britain over the last 150 years. From time to time policy-makers appeared to be near to breaking away from the redundant triangle of punishment–welfare–treatment; their failure to make a clean break resulted in a reluctance to break new ground and an unwillingness to depart from the professional paraphernalia and incarcerative apparatus which dictated policy.

On occasion a bold step is taken which becomes a symbolic inspiration across many countries. The dissolution of incarcerative institutions in Massachusetts, described in Chapter Three, was such a step. Jerry Miller learned and acted rapidly. When appointed state commissioner of youth services in 1969, Miller's intention was to reform the training schools. Less than two years later, finding he had had little success in this endeavour, Miller acted swiftly to close the institutions.

The Massachusetts experience is a rare example of a 'deep end' reform strategy: by first closing institutions Miller forced the development of alternatives in the community. More than a decade later the decarceration process in Massachusetts survives. This is not to say that there are not new problems, and these include controlling the large private agencies which now provide programmes for young people on behalf of the state, and reluctance by professionals to strengthen developmental institutions.

The developmental approach is unlikely to be articulated in policy statements, but it can be identified in practice across a variety of settings; often this practice is far ahead of the language necessary to convey its significance. Chapter Four explores the implications of the developmental approach within the context of the home and school, and looks at ways in which these institutions might be supported and helped, so as to hold on to young people in trouble.

The dangers and shortcomings of a new form of treatment offering less protection than punishment and casting its net even more widely is examined in Chapter Five with reference to the alarming growth in the psychiatric hospitalization of young people in the United States.

In the final chapter it is argued that, once the developmental approach is adopted, problems of policy implementation remain. In particular, attention has to be given to the dynamic and often informal momentum of organizational processes. In conclusion several specific policy recommendations are made.

Chapter Two

Wrong Turnings

I am sure the House will support me in any steps that may be taken to prevent this unnecessary imprisonment. It is an evil which falls only on the sons of the working classes. The sons of other classes may commit many of the same kind of offences and in boisterous and exuberant moments, whether at Oxford or anywhere else, may do things for which the working classes are committed to prison, although injury may not be inflicted on anyone. (Winston S. Churchill, 20 July 1910)

The ideal image of childhood is changing and implies greater precociousness than earlier child savers might have thought possible . . . A decrease in the privileged status of the young, moreover, may bring increased demands for accountability, particularly where criminal acts are involved. Magnified demands for retribution are not an impossibility. (LaMar Empey, 1976, pp. 50–51)

•

Over the last 150 years public policy on young people and crime has remained trapped largely within the triangle of punishment, welfare and treatment. The prominence of any one of these approaches to young people in trouble has varied from time to time, often as a reaction to what has gone before. The perennial issue has been concerned with the type of incarcerative institution rather than with the fundamental principles involved. On occasion an impasse is reached, and an opportunity arises to take a quite different approach. Such opportunities have been rare, and generally have been missed.

Shielding Young People from Punishment, and the Rise of Welfare

Under common law, children under the age of seven were deemed incapable of criminal intent and, between the ages of seven and fourteen, there was a rebuttable presumption that they were not responsible under the law. At the beginning of Queen Victoria's reign children could be punished with imprisonment, transportation and even the death penalty; after all, children were but little adults. As late as 1833, Nicholas White, a nine-year-old, was sentenced to death for the theft of items valued at twopence; the death sentence was commuted to a whipping and transportation for seven years. Two years earlier a thirteen-year-old was executed for the murder of another boy. Similarly, children regularly had transportation sentences commuted to imprisonment. Early efforts to shield children from the full rigours of criminal law were based on notions of diminished responsibility. Later, with the emerging idea of childhood as a period of development, a variety of social reforms sought to protect children from danger and exploitation. In 1847 powers were extended to magistrates' courts to imprison children under the age of fourteen for up to three months. This reform was intended to spare children from prosecution in the higher courts. However, as one contemporary observer noted, the legislation resulted in more rather than fewer children going to prison, providing an early example of the unintended and unanticipated consequences endemic to criminal justice reform.

During the first half of the nineteenth century reformers sought not to repudiate punishment of young children but to restrict its scope. For example, a select committee of the House of Lords regretted any contamination of young people in prison but could suggest only transportation and whipping as alternatives. Policy, if not always practice, within the prison was to separate young people from older prisoners. In

27

1838, Parkhurst prison was established as a specialist prison to hold boys prior to transportation. The opening of Parkhurst was applauded from the standpoint of protecting young prisoners, but by the middle of the century a new approach to dealing with young people and crime was emerging.

Mary Carpenter articulated the welfare approach to a House of Commons committee: 'I have great objection to calling them [i.e. children] even semi-criminal because the word has a moral meaning. I consider the condition they are in as that of extreme neglect' (cited in Manton, 1976, p. 14). Born in 1807, the daughter of a Unitarian minister, Mary Carpenter was a pioneer of free schools for children from economically deprived families. Her first book was entitled *Ragged Schools by a Worker*. Until her death in 1877 she was both practitioner and crusader. A tireless traveller, she lectured extensively in Europe and the United States. In her second book, *Reformatory Schools*, published in 1851, Carpenter suggested that three types of institution were required, namely: for the deprived, free schools; for young vagrants and beggars, industrial schools (day and residential); for convicted youngsters, reformatories under voluntary management. Carpenter's impact on public policy was immense, especially during the period 1850–70 when she campaigned for industrial schools and reformatories. Among her supporters were Mathew Davenport Hill, the recorder of Birmingham, and Charles Adderley, a traditional Tory Member of Parliament. She attacked the boys' prison at Parkhurst in uncompromising terms: 'It is utterly vain to look for any real reformation where the heart is not touched, and where the inner springs of action are not called into healthful exercise; this cannot possibly be done for children under the mechanical and military discipline of Parkhurst' (Carpenter, 1851, p. 322). Parkhurst was unfavourably compared with the private reformatories situated in Surrey and Warwickshire. The first of these, the Philanthropic Society, was founded in London towards the end of the eighteenth century. The absence of surrounding walls gave it claim to be an 'asylum' rather than a prison, and it was intended for 'the destitute children of convicts' and 'for the reform of such young criminals whose youth gave promise of amendment' (cited in Carlebach, 1970, pp. 6–10). In 1849 it was re-established at Redhill with an agricultural basis, and Sidney Turner, the Society's chaplain, became headmaster. The welfare campaign was for legislation to ensure funding and provide institutional managers with powers to detain young people. Mary Carpenter regretted that Parliament had not acted on recent inquiries. Young people

continue to herd in their dens of iniquity, to swarm in our streets, to levy a costly maintenance on the honest and industrious, to rise up to be the parents of a degraded progeny of pauper children, or to people our gaols until they are audaciously wicked enough for transportation – in either case to be a drain on our resources, a festering plague spot to society. (Carpenter, 1851, p. 352)

The welfare reformers of the mid nineteenth century demanded that children be removed from the prison system and placed in privately managed but state-assisted institutions. These institutions would also rescue other young people from corrupting environments. Persistent lobbying led to statutory provision for reformatories in 1854 and industrial schools in 1857. The result was rapidly to increase the total number of young persons in institutions. The expansion of institutions proceeded at a phenomenal rate. By 1858, only four years after the enabling legislation, there were forty-five reformatories holding 2,000 young people. Twelve years later there were sixty-five reformatories and fifty industrial schools holding 7,000 young people. By the end of the century the number of young people held in these institutions increased more than threefold.

It was not until the last few years of her life that Mary Carpenter displayed any doubts about the utility of the reformatory movement. She was aware that many of these incarcerative institutions were not steeped in her non-punitive ideas. In her final years she turned her attention to day industrial schools, opening one herself in 1872. Two years later she was arguing that it was totally wrong to remove children from their families unless absolutely necessary: 'We should not sever the family ties of all these young persons, or place the hand of the policeman on so many thousands of the rising generation. Nor should we remove from local School Boards, elected and supported by the people, the responsibility of these children' (cited in Manton, 1976, p. 231). Carpenter had finally acknowledged the importance of the home and school.

Although in 1876 Carpenter was able to gain statutory authority for School Boards to maintain day industrial schools, these institutions were fragile and short-lived. Mary Carpenter's legacy was not day schools but the incarcerative industrial schools and reformatories which became approved schools in 1933 and community homes with education on the premises in 1969. The welfare approach sprang from an educational framework, preceding the Education Act 1870:

It is wonderful how soon a master who is well trained in the art of teaching will introduce discipline in the most disorderly assemblage of children, and quicken into intelligence those who before seemed dead to all but animal pleasures. To know how and when to loosen the rein to the wild and hitherto uncurbed creature, and yet make him feel, almost without knowing it, that there is a bound which he must not pass. (Carpenter, 1851, p. 108)

Mary Carpenter was a pioneer in her regard for the school as a developmental institution. Her support for compulsory school attendance went far beyond the provision of a rudimentary education. The work at the beginning and end of her life, with free and day industrial schools respectively, was the antithesis of the incarcerative institutions for which she is remembered.

The failure by welfare reformers to exploit the educational basis of their work was made evident by the early control gained by the Home Office over the new industrial schools. The Act of 1857 had established that industrial schools would be certified by the Committee of the Privy Council on Education, rather than the Home Office. However, three years later control passed to the Home Office. The rationale for this move was:

There is no moral or social difference between the classes of children who fill the reformatories on the one hand, or the industrial schools on the other. It may be right to place in different establishments those who have broken the law by positive crime and those who have been found guilty of nothing worse than vagrancy; but it must be a matter of accident under which of these two heads the committal of a child takes place; and after committal there can be no substantial difference in the treatment and discipline which they severally require. (Cited in Lushington, 1896, p. 318)

The transfer to the Home Office anticipated the notion of 'net widening'. It was argued that an educational emphasis would encourage incarceration in order to provide an education otherwise not available. Ten years before passage of the Education Act, which provided a national framework for elementary education, this concern may have had some justification:

There is a constant tendency to treat simple poverty or the neglect of parents, as a sufficient reason for placing a child in a certified industrial school, who thus becomes chargeable to the taxes, in relief either of its parents or of the poor rate. Abuses of this kind easily pass current under the name of education. The responsibility of parents is hardly attempted to be enforced by the managers and it may be said, generally, that an education department, appointed to assist voluntary effort, is, of all others, the least adapted to check such irregularities. (Cited in Lushington, 1896, p. 318)

31

It might have been expected that, with the passage of the Education Act 1870, the authority over industrial schools would have been returned to the Education Department. This was not to be, although an attempt was made the following year by Charles Adderley, who had sponsored the original reformatory legislation but, by now, was distressed by the incarcerative nature of the new institutions. Sydney Turner, Home Office Inspector of Schools since leaving Redhill in 1857, lobbied strongly against such a move. After being visited by Adderley, Turner wrote to the Home Secretary that: '. . . it has always seemed to me as a matter of social policy to make a clear distinction between the honest and dishonest classes of society, and it would be a great injustice to the well-behaved and well brought up child to confound it in any respect with the lawless and disorderly . . .' Turner was at pains to stress the similarities between industrial schools and reformatories, commenting that industrial schools are '. . . but reformatories of a milder type', containing 'ragged and neglected classes' (cited in Lushington, 1896, p. 319).

By the early 1880s Adderley's disillusion with reformatories and industrial schools was complete, and he urged that they be replaced by 'schools for neglected and destitute children' (cited in Carlebach, 1970, p. 75). Despite the intentions of the welfare reformers only two decades earlier, the institutional regimes had become penal and restrictive, all the more so given rising social standards in the general community. Home Office inspectors frequently were appalled by what they encountered. The institutional managers, preoccupied by sheer financial survival, were encouraged by the per capita payment by central government to admit very young children and to hold them for the full five-year period. Concerns regarding central government's lack of fiscal and management control prompted the establishment of a Royal Commission in 1883, but the multitude of emerging difficulties were beyond its competence. However, within a decade there were to be two important initiatives by the Home Office.

Crossroads at the turn of the century

Herbert Asquith, the Home Secretary in William Gladstone's third administration, set up two departmental committees on the penal system. The first of these, chaired by Herbert Gladstone, the Parliamentary Under Secretary, reported on the prison system in April 1895. The following year another committee, chaired by Sir Godfrey Lushington, reported on reformatory and industrial schools. The Gladstone report is remembered for elevating treatment, as a purpose for the prison system, alongside punishment. In particular, the report stressed that reformative efforts be made with younger prisoners, and the foundation was created for the borstal system. In essence, Gladstone gave legitimacy to the view that custody might be a positive experience. The idea of treatment within prison had arrived.

A central figure with respect to both committees was Sir Godfrey Lushington, who, in early 1895, had retired as Permanent Secretary of the Home Office. Lushington was born in 1832, the son of Stephen Lushington, an early prison reformer who was for thirty years a progressive member of parliament. In 1869 Lushington was appointed as counsel to the Home Office and in 1885 became its permanent head.

In his evidence to the Gladstone committee Lushington explicitly rejected the emerging treatment approach. In doing so, Lushington eloquently described the reality of prison:

I regard as unfavourable to reformation the status of a prisoner throughout his whole career; the crushing of self-respect; the starving of all moral instinct he may possess; the absence of all opportunity to do or receive a kindness; the continual association with none but criminals, and that only as a separate item amongst other items also separate; the forced labour and the denial of all liberty. I believe the true mode of reforming a man or restoring him to society is exactly in the opposite direction of all these. But, of course, this is a mere idea. It is quite impracticable in a prison. In fact, the unfavourable features I have mentioned are inseparable from a prison life. All that I care to insist on is that this treatment is not reformatory. I consider that a medieval thief who had his right hand chopped off was much more likely to turn over a new leaf than a convict who has had 10 years penal servitude.

Godfrey Lushington detailed his objection to treatment within the prison with particular reference to young people:

I am entirely against the imprisonment of children under 16: but I may say not for the reason usually given. I do not believe in actual contamination inside the prison. The younger prisoners are exercised apart from the elder ones, and there can be no real conversation between them. The actual mischief which comes from juveniles being in prison is, no doubt, what has been pointed out, namely, their possible after recognition by the older prisoners when they come out; but though this may lead to the ruin of certain individual prisoners, I am rather incredulous about its being carried out in a large scale. However, my objection to the imprisonment of young persons is that imprisonment is at once not severe enough, and too severe. It is not severe enough because boys at this age make light of a short period of imprisonment. Unlike their elders, they are accustomed to be ordered about; they do not mind discomfort and hardship. They have no anxiety for their family being impoverished, and no power of looking forward or realizing the after effects of imprisonment. On the other hand, the punishment is, in its subsequent consequences, far too severe. The boys, when they grow up, carry through life the stigma of having been in prison, perhaps only for a freak of mischief; and they get to think of themselves in association with crime and criminals, which is bad for them, in some cases depressing to them, in other cases stimulating them to criminal exploits.

It followed that Lushington explicitly rejected the proposal being canvassed for a 'penal reformatory'. His forthright comments anticipated a developmental approach:

The idea of a government reformatory, I think, is that boys might be subjected to a long course of penal treatment without the stigma of having been in prison. Now, in the first place, I believe that the stigma would attach to this penal reformatory just as much as it does now to an ordinary reformatory or even to a gaol. There is some stigma attaching now to reformatory boys; they are not allowed to enter the Navy at all, and there is often difficulty found in disposing of them in any respectable calling or in any respectable service. Then, which is a stronger objection in my mind, prolonged penal treatment, I consider, is wholly unsuited for boys, thoroughly bad for them. What father would think of keeping his son in disgrace for two or three years? It seems to be a completely unnatural and inappropriate treatment. On the contrary, what is wanted is kindness and encouragement. Ordinary reformatories profess not to be penal at all, but of course they are penal, they cannot help being so, and I think they are a great deal too much so. The isolation, the monotony, the complete dependence of life, and the want of all the free play of society in general – these must be terribly penal to a young boy, and, in my mind, they constitute very serious drawbacks to the reformatory system.

The chairman of the committee pressed Lushington further on the idea of a penal reformatory:

We have had evidence to show, at least statements have been made to show, that the habitual criminal is created practically between the ages of 16 and 21 as a rule. If any establishment could be organized in the nature of a prison, but which was specially adapted for the teaching of industrial work; and at any rate for giving a great deal of agricultural work and land reclamation work to them, do not you think that such a prison might possibly succeed with a certain number of these young offenders who simply have turned out habitual offenders by the present prison system as it is?

Lushington: That is not my view. I do not like prisons much, but in some respects I prefer them to reformatories, that is to say, I would far rather send a lad of 17 or 18 to a comparatively brief term of imprisonment than I would shut him up in a reformatory between 18 and 21, which I believe is now what many of the reformatory managers are asking for. In my opinion, when a boy has been free up till 16, he is too old to bend himself to the severe discipline of reformatory life, for the first time imposed upon him; and it is in my judgement entirely wrong that lads from 18 to 21, who are really young men, should be treated like children, have everything ordered for them, and in case of disobedience should be liable to be flogged. Such treatment is not likely to turn them out good useful men, or make them inclined to do their duty to the community. I should say that proposals to this effect coming from reformatory managers, ought to be very carefully scrutinized. As it is, reformatory managers notoriously keep the boys too long . . . It is, of course, to the interest of managers to keep their reformatories full, and also to have the profit from the remunerative labour of the older boys . . .

One member of the committee, Sir Algernon West, attempted to persuade Lushington that Redhill might be regarded as a school:

West: Do you know yourself personally anything as to the conduct of the Redhill reformatory?

Lushington: I know a little about it; I read the evidence which has been given.

West: It is rather on the same principle as our large public schools. There are separate houses, and it is conducted very much the same as a large public school, and I certainly say the percentage of boys there who turn out well and lead honest lives is much greater than they would be at any of the public schools, because I think they said that they amount to 93 per cent of the boys that go there. I was tremendously impressed with Redhill.

Lushington: I do not accept those statistics without qualification.

West: No, I suppose not.

Lushington: First of all it assumes that all the boys, because they were convicted boys, would turn out ill. That is, I think, a large assumption; and in the next place it assumes that the whole of that long detention has been necessary to secure their reformation. But I quite concur with you that, as far as I know, the system of conducting the Redhill reformatory is the right one, that is to say, that boys of different ages are separated and not more than a certain number of boys are collected under the same roof, so that there is some possibility of giving them personal attention. But when you compare them with our public schools, I recollect that schoolboys have four months holidays in the year, when they are with their fathers and mothers, and brothers and sisters. I think there is a very great difference there.

West: I did not quite mean it was the same, but I meant the system was the same of separate boarding houses, separate messing, and having their amusements separate in each house. In each house they have their football matches and so on?

Lushington: Yes.

                                        (Gladstone, 1895, pp. 401–3)

The thrust of Lushington's evidence was not accepted by the Gladstone committee. No recommendation was made by the committee to bar juveniles from prison. Instead the committee recommended that juveniles (the age, it considered, should be raised to include sixteen-year-olds) be kept quite separate and be subject to special reformatory efforts. The committee did not share Lushington's disdain for a penal reformatory and recommended that the government should experiment with the idea. The committee believed that the new treatment approach should be located within the prison system, declaring: 'The penal reformatory should be a half-way house between the prison and the reformatory.'

There is some irony that the Gladstone committee's enthusiasm for a treatment initiative within the prison system was partly based upon a report of 1893 describing the Elmira reformatory in New York state. The committee members appear to have been blissfully unaware that when they began their deliberations the Elmira reformatory had just been subjected to an intensive inquiry concerning allegations of widespread brutality. It was the stated purposes, rather than the realities, of the Elmira regime which attracted international attention including that of the Gladstone committee.

Elmira's purposes were consistent with the Declaration of Principles agreed upon at the National Congress on Penitentiaries and Reformatory Discipline in 1870. Zebulon Brockway, appointed as the first superintendent of Elmira in 1876, had a hand in drafting the Declaration which reflected an enthusiastic endorsement of the treatment approach to youth crime. Brockway's stated objective was to make Elmira as little like an ordinary prison and so much like a college or hospital'. But everyday life at Elmira was very different. Brockway was an early pioneer in penological linguistics. He referred to solitary confinement as 'rest cure cells' and to corporal punishment as 'positive extraneous assistance'. In 1894 the New York State Board of Charities found that: 'The charges and allegations against the general superintendent Z. R. Brockway, of "cruel, brutal, excessive and unusual punishment of the inmates" are proven and most amply sustained by the evidence.' The evidence showed that Brockway '. . . whipped prisoners, punched inmates in the face, hit them over the head with the whip's handle, placed prisoners on bread and water, handcuffed them to their cell doors for up to 14 hours a day, and even suspended them from a rope and pulley in the bathroom' (Pisciotta, 1983, p. 624). Although political machinations led to Brockway's exoneration, in 1900, following a change of state governor, he was finally pressured into resigning.

In 1896 the new head of the English prison system, Evelyn Ruggles-Brise, visited both Elmira and the Concord reformatory in Massachusetts. Ruggles-Brise endorsed the general principle rather than the actual practice he observed in the United States. He viewed the penal reformatory as having its heritage less in the United States than in reformatories such as Redhill. Cautiously, in 1900 the Prison Commission began to experiment at Bedford prison and, two years later, at the prison in the village of Borstal, near Rochester.

In May 1895, a month after the Gladstone committee reported, Asquith set up a departmental committee under Sir Godfrey Lushington to examine reformatory and industrial schools. The committee visited over 200 institutions (including day industrial schools and working boys' homes) and took extensive evidence. The report and some of the dissenting memoranda, most of them signed by Lushington, provided an extraordinary challenge to orthodoxy. There was agreement that there was little difference between industrial schools and reformatories other than the age of the inmates: 'In a reformatory the inmates are older, and older means more criminal . . .' Furthermore the committee rejected the view (pressed on them by the Home Office Inspector, J. G. Legge, formerly of the Prison Commission, and secretary to the Gladstone committee) that young people in the institutions could be distinguished from ordinary children on physical and mental characteristics and disagreed that their educational needs differed. Indeed the report urged that ' . . . education should embrace the entire nature and entire life of the child and, moreover, should regard the child not merely as an individual, but also as a member of a family and of society'. The report implied that, had the educational rationale been better understood thirty or forty years before, the extensive growth of incarcerative institutions might have been avoided.

From its visits to institutions the committee contrasted constructive and repressive regimes, comparing ' . . . the system of confidence, which seeks to allow liberty so far as it may be safe to do so, with a view to influencing the child and encouraging a sense of responsibility' and 'a system of securing obedience by watching and repression'. However, the core of the report questioned the wisdom of placing young people in institutions at all. The committee challenged the 'asylum theory' subscribed to by 'many magistrates' which assumed that 'sending the child away is best for the child'. Indeed, the asylum theory was soundly rejected: 'Nothing short of necessity can justify detention in one of these schools.' Any positive features of institutions had to be balanced against

the evils, by no means so obvious, which are inherent in institutional life, notwithstanding the best intentions of those in charge of the institutions, the risk that the child may come out unchanged, or unable to earn its livelihood, or be 'returned to friends' or the possibility that the child may be made worse by the companions worse than itself, whom it finds in the school; and the stigma, such as it is, of having been in an industrial school.

Encouraged by reports of successful boarding out by Dr Barnardo, the committee recommended that more use be made of boarding out and specifically recommended: 'Boarding out to be authorized as an alternative to commitment to an industrial school, and in the case of a child under 10, to be adopted in preference and if not adopted the court to report the case to the Secretary of State.'

The driving force behind the committee's radical challenge to orthodoxy was Godfrey Lushington. Lushington would have liked the committee to have gone further, but he was unable to carry all his colleagues with him. Lushington joined with others in three notes-of-dissent memoranda which further reflected a developmental approach. The case was put for boarding out as an alternative to institutions. The argument against institutions was also given greater emphasis. These difficulties 'are stated because they seldom get discussed'. Lushington and his dissenting colleagues stated:

The object recognized is that by the end of the time the boy may be qualified to take his place in society, in other words, may have become like boys in general, not merely honest and indisposed to commit crime, but – so far as the case may admit, free both in his own mind and in the estimate of others from association with crime, and with a portion of the common qualities that go to make up a worthy and effective member of a family and subject of the state, such as self-respect, self-control, self-reliance, diligence, and again, regard for others, affectionate-ness, public spirit. It is admitted that anything like penal or humiliating treatment to continue after the space of three or four or more years would be inconsistent with such an object, besides being harsh and unjust. The work is manifestly a work of education in the broadest sense of that term.

They viewed with distress the escalating increase in the number of institutions which then held 24,000 young people; their position was stated precisely: 'What is required is not expansion, but reduction.' Lushington also joined with others to argue that responsibility for the institutions should be transferred from the Home Office to the Department of Education with the aim 'to assimilate them more and more to ordinary schools, and to treat the inmates as children at other schools are treated, and not as a class apart'. Firmly opposed to Lushington were four members of the committee including Sir John Dorrington M P, who had served on the Gladstone committee and was a former chairman of Gloucester Quarter Sessions, and a clergyman who disassociated himself from the report in its entirety. The Dorrington faction argued against boarding out and took a favourable view of incarcer-ative institutions.

The implications of the Gladstone and Lushington reports pointed in quite different directions. Gladstone stressed that treatment was achievable in the prison setting, especially with respect to young adults. Gladstone wished to retain the Home Office role, preferring a dual system with 'adult reformatories' run by the Prison Commission alongside reformatories inspected by the Home Office but locally man-aged. In contrast, Lushington pointed towards alternatives to

41

incarceration and sought remedies to youth crime within the home and the school as much as from criminal justice. Gladstone sought to legitimize the incarcerative institution, while Lushington sketched a bold alternative course, but one which was trodden only tentatively during the century to follow.

Twentieth-Century Drift and Muddle

The nineteenth century opened with punishment as the single approach to young people and crime. By the 1850s the welfare idea was making a strong challenge and, as the century closed, the treatment approach had also arrived. The importance of the Gladstone and Lushington committees was to articulate the nature of the policy choices. Lushington warned against endowing institutions with either a welfare or a treatment ideology. The dismal history of industrial schools and reformatories was testimony to the mistaken direction taken by welfare reformers. By rejecting the 'penal reformatory', Lushington warned that the treatment ideology ultimately provided yet another rationale for incarcerative institutions. A different approach was required if punishment was to be displaced.

During the nineteenth century welfare reformers sought the removal of young people from the prison system by establishing new types of institution. To a considerable extent the new institutions replaced the prison system, but they had also incarcerated many young people whose involvement in crime was slight or non-existent. Events during the twentieth century confirmed that welfare and treatment rationales all too easily lead to further incarceration.

1906–18

In 1906 a reforming Liberal administration took office and quickly legislated on young people and crime. In 1907 the Probation of Offenders Act was enacted, followed the next year by the Children Act and the Prevention of Crime Act. The legislative activity mainly reflected the aims of welfare reformers. The Children Act barred under-fourteens from prison and provided that 14–15 year olds could only go to prison if the court issued an 'unruly' certificate. These measures were offset by a new short-term sentence of detention of periods of up to one month. These sentences were to be served in remand homes run by the police. The Act is best known for establishing juvenile courts, although in several cities juvenile courts had already been unofficially established. Under the legislation the juvenile court was to sit at different times from the regular court and, with some exceptions, had powers to hear all charges other than of murder.

Despite urging by welfare reformers and the Gladstone committee, the Children Act did not increase the upper age limit of entrance to reformatories from sixteen to eighteen. However, provisions for 'borstal' institutions were included in the Prevention of Crime Act 1908. The sentence to borstal was to be for from one to three years (with powers of release after six months) for persons aged between sixteen and twenty, with powers for the age limit to be increased to twenty-three by order. The new institution was intended for a person where 'by reason of his criminal habits and tendencies or associations with persons of such character, it is expedient that he should be subject to detention for such a term and under such instruction and discipline as appears most conducive to his reformation and the repression of crime'. Herbert Gladstone was Home Secretary, and it is not surprising that he sought to implement one of the main proposals made by his committee thirteen years earlier.

Lushington's warning against the penal reformatory was disregarded, and the treatment approach to the young adult was to be attempted within the prison system. However, a further thirteen years elapsed before any real effort was made to create a distinctive borstal regime.

The Probation of Offenders Act endorsed the principle of holding offenders under supervision within the community. The Act consolidated and extended arrangements which had developed informally and had been encouraged by legislation over the previous quarter of a century. The 1907 legislation encouraged the employment of probation officers, but this provision did not become obligatory for courts until 1925. The focus of early probation practice was on young people, and by 1920 four out of every five of the 10,000 people under probation supervision were under twenty-one. The increased use by the courts of probation supervision contributed to the dramatic drop in the number of young people held in reformatories and industrial schools during the first two decades of the century. At the turn of the century there were 24,000 young people held in these institutions, but by 1913 the numbers were down to 19,000 and by 1922 had fallen even more sharply to 8,000. About forty institutions were closed in the five or six years immediately after the First World War. Indeed, Sir Edward Troup, one of Lushington's successors, regretted that young people were being placed on probation who, in his opinion, would have been better sent to institutions (Troup, 1925, p. 140). Within the Children's Branch of the Home Office, which had been established in 1913, there was speculation that the decline in institutional numbers resulted from, in addition to the impact of probation orders, a reluctance by local authorities to meet the costs of institutions, the wider educational provision (the school-leaving age was raised to fourteen in 1918) and a widespread scepticism about institutions in general.

1922–39

During the first two decades of the century little was done to steer borstals clear of the punishment approach. By the early 1920s public disquiet about brutality within borstals followed critical articles in segments of the media. The conditions were right for a different approach. The appointment of Alexander Paterson as a member of the Prison Commission ensured that the new direction would be one of welfare/treatment and that the borstal system would be rescued. Paterson's famous dictum, that men could not be trained for freedom in conditions of captivity, was an argument for liberalized prison and borstal regimes, not for alternatives to incarceration. As a former social worker in Bermondsey and a critic of the prison system, Paterson was an unlikely choice as prison commissioner. Brought in by Sir Maurice Waller, the new head of the prison system, Paterson's mandate was to give borstals the sort of distinctive regime which had been envisaged almost thirty years earlier by the Gladstone committee. As Roger Hood has noted, with Paterson's appointment an infusion of new ideas and personnel 'gradually increased the prestige of borstal, and further emphasized its detachment from penal roots' (Hood, 1965, p. 32). The attacks subsided as Paterson presented borstals in the image of the public school. Borstal officers came out of uniform and housemasters and matrons were recruited. In 1925 Paterson informed the readers of *The Times*, 'Borstals combine many of the features of a public school . . . with a long day's industrial training and strict discipline.' Paterson rejected brute force and mindless uniformity as training methods, believing

the springs of action lie deeper than the laws of habit or the voice of the mentor are likely to reach . . . the most difficult way of training a lad is to regard him as a living organism, having its secret of life and motive-power within . . . if an officer can, without losing his balance, control and common sense, treat his lads as he would treat working lads in a rough club outside, the great majority will rise to the suggestions and live up to the level on which they have been set. (Cited in Ruck, 1951, pp. 97–9)

In January 1925 a Home Office committee was set up to examine the 'treatment' and 'protection' of young offenders up to the age of twenty-one. The chairman was Sir Thomas Malony, who had been Lord Chief Justice of Ireland until 1924, and the committee members included Sir Maurice Waller. Most of the sixty-five recommendations of the Malony committee, which reported in March 1927, pointed in a welfare/treatment direction. These included raising the age of criminal responsibility from seven to eight and the upper age limit of the juvenile court from sixteen to seventeen and, in the light of experience, perhaps to eighteen. The Malony report failed to capitalize on the general scepticism about institutions of the early 1920s. It had little to say about industrial schools and reformatories other than recommending they be merged to become approved schools.

The committee believed that the 1,700 young people sent to prison each year could be dealt with by either borstal or probation. Paterson urged the committee to recommend that borstal be used at an early stage in a young person's offending career. The report implied that there was a need for more than the three existing borstal institutions. Remand centres were recommended as another means of keeping young people out of prison. The committee decided that there was 'no sufficient reason for making any fundamental change in the legal principle underlying the juvenile court'. It urged, however, that 'the welfare of the child or young person should be the primary object of the juvenile court'. The principle that young people were not only to be dealt with separately from adults but in a way that promoted their best interests was given expression in the Children and Young Persons Act 1933.

The ambivalence to the punishment approach by members of the Malony committee was apparent. The majority would not accept the view of three members that judicial corporal punishment for 14–16 year old boys should be ended. On the other hand, the committee rejected the proposal by the Magistrates' Association, which had been founded in 1921, that a new short-term institutional sentence be available to the courts. The committee viewed such a sentence as being undesirable especially when it interfered with school attendance: 'The establishment of short-term schools without definitive evidence as to the need for them and as to their success would in our opinion be open to grave risk.' The Malony committee preferred that investment be made in hostels and the idea of the detention centre, unapologetically punitive in approach, had to wait until 1948 for legislative endorsement.

The Children and Young Persons Act of 1933 incorporated much of what the Malony committee had to say concerning persons up to the age of seventeen. The legislation did not, however, bar sixteen-year-olds from borstal as the committee had recommended. For Paterson a satisfactory outcome of the Malony report was that it paved the way for an expansion of the borstal system. By 1933 there were eight borstals, and two more were added in 1938. In 1936 the maximum age for a borstal sentence was raised from twenty to twenty-two.* Borstals were the only part of the prison system to expand during the inter-war years. The Gladstone committee's notion of a penal reformatory located within but somehow distinct from the rest of the prison system had finally come to fruition. In 1928 a borstal governor said the young men 'looked forward to a time when the traditions of Borstal would be at

* The maximum age was reduced to twenty by the Criminal Justice Act 1948.

least equal to those of Eton and Harrow' (cited in Hood, 1965, pp. 53–4). A decade or so later the well-known magistrate John Watson was still insisting: 'First and foremost Borstal is *not* a prison. To describe a Borstal institution as a prison for older boys and girls is scarcely more accurate than to describe an approved school as a prison for children.' For good measure, Watson added: 'For the boy or girl with whom all else has failed Borstal is not the end; it is a new beginning' (Watson, 1942, pp. 158–61).

During the 1930s, along with borstal sentences there was an increased use of other types of institution for young people. Approved-school numbers rose, as did the number of youngsters sentenced to detention in remand homes.* By the mid-1930s there were signs of a revitalized emphasis on punishment as the rationale for institutional usage. In particular the Magistrates' Association were at pains to keep alive their sentencing idea of 'young offenders detention', which argued that detention was needed to occupy the ground on the tariff between probation and borstal. Further support came in March 1938 from the departmental committee on corporal punishment:

If, as we recommend, corporal punishment is abolished, further consideration should be given to the question of strengthening the authority of the Juvenile Courts by conferring on them some additional powers to enable them to deal more effectively with those cases which do not call for any form of training or other remedial measures but require merely some form of punishment which will operate effectively as a deterrent. (Cadogan, 1938, p. 49)

Ironically, supporters of the punishment approach were frustrated by the Conservative government of the day. Among the sources of their frustration was the appointment, by Neville Chamberlain in May 1937, of Sir Samuel Hoare as

* Usage fell between 1910 and 1933 (from 360 to none) but by 1939 was at 200 and continued to climb steadily during the war, and in 1949 was 700. (See Radzinowicz, 1952, pp. 2–3.)

Home Secretary. Hoare was great-great-grandson of the Samuel Hoare who was brother-in-law to both Elizabeth Fry and Sir Fowell Buxton, with whom, in 1816, he founded the Society for the Reformation of Prison Discipline. Hoare later wrote: 'The thought of carrying on this tradition made a very strong appeal to me' (Templewood, 1954, p. 224). Quickly he had decided upon far-reaching legislation: 'My advisors, seeing my interest in penal questions, entered heart and soul into the prospect of a comprehensive criminal justice bill that was long overdue.' In November he circulated his general proposals to the cabinet, and twelve months later the bill received its second reading.

The main clauses included:

- An end to the imprisonment of persons under sixteen, and restrictions on the imprisonment of persons aged between sixteen and twenty. It was proposed that powers of imprisonment for this age group be removed from the lower courts. These provisions were to take effect once new sentencing alternatives were in place. Remand centres were to be established.
- Attendance centres (sixty hours over six months) for persons aged between twelve and twenty-one.
- 'Howard Houses' for young persons aged between sixteen and twenty-one. The maximum length of stay was to be six months with a six-months' supervision. It was envisaged that residents would be closely supervised but would obtain work outside the house.
- The abolition of judicial corporal punishment. This was the most controversial part of the bill, and it is by no means certain that Hoare would have got this section through the House of Commons.

It is significant that the bill did not include short-term custodial sentences, thereby rejecting one of the main demands of the Magistrates' Association. Hoare preferred to follow the Malony committee and to set up hostels in the community rather than punishment-oriented institutions. Hoare was in the mainstream of the liberal optimism which Paterson had brought to the topic of dealing with young people and crime. The essence of Hoare's bill was to remove young people from prisons to less harsh parts of the prison system. Hoare was also anxious to strengthen the role of the probation service, which by the mid-1930s was responsible for about one half of all children and young persons found guilty of indictable offences.

The bill was abandoned in November 1939 because of wartime pressures on Parliament. By 1947, when Parliament returned to the matter, there was a new enthusiasm for the punishment approach. In that same year Alexander Paterson died, closing an era characterized by efforts to make incarceration a positive experience. Paterson was in the tradition of Gladstone rather than Lushington. He believed that the treatment approach could be congruent with custody. The logic of Lushington pointed in a different direction, towards thinking in terms of the context, the stigma, and the social and personal consequences of the incarcerative institution. By contrast, Paterson was a programme person, believing that with the right staff great things could be achieved. Paterson wished to loosen the penal connection but not to sever it. Despite his early work among the poor of London, Paterson showed little interest in developmental institutions. He failed to build upon one of the most promising features of the borstal system, namely the involvement of the several hundred voluntary after-care associates. These persons were used to support young people after their release from borstal. Had Paterson followed the logic of Lushington he might have advocated use of this resource as an alternative instead of as an appendage to borstal.

1945–60

The clamour for a punishment approach to young people and crime gathered steam during the Second World War. For example, in 1942 John Watson, widely regarded as a progressive juvenile court chairman, called for a new type of incarceration which provided a 'short sharp punishment to bring the offender to his senses and as a deterrent in future'. Watson elaborated his concept:

What is needed is a small local establishment in which the discipline is of the sternest, the food of the plainest, where everything is done 'at the double', and where there is the maximum of hard work and the minimum of amusement: the kind of establishment a young offender would not wish to visit twice, and of which he would paint a vivid picture on his return home. (Watson, 1942, p. 143)

In September 1944 the Home Secretary, Herbert Morrison, set up an Advisory Council on the Treatment of Offenders under the chairmanship of Mr Justice Birkett with the Permanent Secretary of the Home Office as deputy chairman. The Council's first task was to review the provisions of the 1938 bill with a view to renewed legislation. The Magistrates' Association renewed their demands for a new short-term custodial sentence and the Advisory Council was persuaded to endorse this idea, which, in turn, was accepted by the Labour government and found a place in the new bill. The Home Secretary, Chuter Ede, told the House of Commons: 'There is a type of offender to whom it is necessary to give a short, but sharp reminder that he is getting into ways that will inevitably lead him into disaster . . . Their regime will consist of brisk discipline and hard work.'

The contrast between 1938 and 1948 is unexpected. In 1938 a Conservative Home Secretary rejected the notion of the detention centre, pressed on him by the Cadogan committee and the Magistrates' Association. Ten years later a

51

Labour Home Secretary accepted the detention centre idea, pressed on him by the Advisory Council and the Magistrates' Association. As in 1938, the essence of the legislation was to remove young people from prison but not from the prison system. Magistrates' courts were barred from sending anyone under seventeen to prison, and higher courts anyone under fifteen, and both were required to give reasons for imprisoning anyone under twenty-one. As recommended by the Malony committee twenty years earlier, remand centres were to be provided within the prison system. The 1948 Act gave less emphasis than Hoare's bill to non-institutional sanctions. The attendance centre sentence was reduced to a maximum of twelve hours because the detention centre was intended to deal with those requiring longer punishment. The proposed Howard Houses were dropped. Instead, the Home Office was empowered to give grants to voluntary bodies to set up probation hostels.*

The punishment mood of the 1940s cast its shadow over the next decade. In particular, the process began to reintegrate borstals into the prison system. A special punishment borstal was established in 1950, and two years later a Home Office committee recommended harsher regimes throughout the borstal system. In 1961 a new sentencing framework essentially removed the distinctive sentencing features of borstal, reinforcing what had taken place at the level of penal practice. In 1960 a criminologist, Gordon Rose, complained about the absence of innovation within borstals, prompting a colleague to comment: 'While reformatory treatment for young offenders retains its penal connections there is probably little hope that it will make the strides which Dr. Rose suggests' (Hood, 1965, p. 160). However,

---

* Writing in 1954, Hoare had little to say about the differences between his bill and the Criminal Justice Act of 1948, describing them as 'almost identical'. He made no mention of Howard Houses and he curiously implied that detention centres originated in his bill.

Paterson's efforts to loosen the penal connections of borstals had been firmly reversed.

In 1960 the Ingleby committee rejected any merger of approved schools with other residential provision or the removal of responsibility for these institutions from the Home Office. The following year the minimum age for borstal sentencing was reduced from sixteen to fifteen. In large part this was due to lobbying by approved-school staff who wished to be more easily rid of their most troublesome youngsters.

The 1950s closed with the Ingleby committee, which was set up in 1956 and in its report of 1960, endorsed the structure of the juvenile court. Indeed, the committee suggested that the juvenile court be strengthened with powers to sentence directly to borstal. While the Ingleby report accepted the status quo, it did propose raising the age of criminal responsibility from eight to twelve, thereby replacing criminal with welfare procedures. As Ingleby put it: 'A child under the age would no longer be liable to be prosecuted and convicted, but he could still commit offences; the law would prescribe a new way in which he should come before the court' (Ingleby, 1960, p. 36). In 1963, as a legislative compromise, the age of criminal responsibility was raised to ten.

Although provided for by the Criminal Justice Act 1948, the first detention centre was not opened until 1952.* The Magistrates' Association led the campaign for the extension of detention centres across the country. With the prison-building programme announced in the 1959 white paper *Penal Practice in a Changing Society*, there was renewed urgency for the construction of both detention and remand centres.

---

* Under the Criminal Justice Act 1948 powers to sentence juveniles to periods of up to one month in a remand home were to be removed as detention centres became available.

1964–70

The period since the Second World War has been dominated by the punishment approach, except for six years or so during the 1960s which were characterized by a brief renaissance of welfare/treatment optimism. There was disappointment with the Ingleby report and an expectation that a future Labour government would be more bold. Chaired by Lord Longford, a Labour Party review of criminal justice, reporting just a few months before the election of 1964, called for the replacement of the juvenile court with new procedures providing treatment 'without any stigma'. When Labour came to power in October 1964, work began on a white paper encompassing both juveniles and young adults. Published in 1965, *The Child, The Family and the Young Offender* provoked an immediate and hostile reaction. In particular the proposal to increase the age of criminal responsibility to sixteen and to replace juvenile courts with a system of family councils and family courts led to virulent opposition by the Magistrates' Association and, to a lesser extent, by some probation officers. There are several curious features to the 1965 white paper. In focusing on abolition of the juvenile court and setting up a special court for 16–20 year olds, the white paper left existing sanctions intact. Senior approved schools were to be incorporated into the prison system by merger with borstals. The welfare reformers of a century earlier would have been astounded by the fate of their reformatory ideal. Another curious aspect of the white paper was its studied disregard of significant proposals which had been published north of the border. The Kilbrandon committee, which had reported in April 1964, described the task of dealing with young people in trouble as being one of 'education for social living'. Kilbrandon rejected punishment measures as not being compatible with the nature of the educational process itself. Kilbrandon was in the developmental tradition of Godfrey Lushington seventy years earlier:

The principle underlying the present range of treatment measures is . . . primarily an educational one, in the sense that it is intended, wherever possible, not to supersede the natural beneficial influences of the home and the family, but wherever practicable to strengthen, support and supplement them in situations in which for whatever reason they have been weakened or have failed in their effect. (Kilbrandon, 1964, p. 20)

At least one commentator has suggested that the Kilbrandon committee shrewdly presented their strategy in education rather than treatment/welfare terms (Bruce, 1982, p. 7). But over the next year or so Scottish social workers succeeded in recasting 'education for social living' in the ideology of professional social work. The Scottish legislation of 1968 entrusted social workers rather than education departments with the task of implementing the children's panels and other new procedures. Kilbrandon commented later that he did not regret the shift away from the educational emphasis:

I do not regret that the Committee's idea of attaching the children's panels, and the supporting field organization, to the education authorities was rejected in favour of the Social Work system as we know it. I do not mean that intellectually or fundamentally we were wrong, but rather that the organizational difficulties would have led to much opposition and frustration. (Kilbrandon, 1976, p. lx)

The rejection of punishment in the Kilbrandon report was forthright: 'We do not believe that a retention of the present system, resting as it does on an attempt to retain the two existing concepts in harness, is susceptible of modification in any way which would seem likely to make any real impact on the problem' (p. 40). Punishment was regarded as being 'ultimately incompatible with the nature of the educational process itself' (Kilbrandon, 1964, p. 20).

The central weakness of the English white paper of 1965

compared with the Scottish proposals was the absence of a carefully argued rationale. The authors were in some difficulty, as there was little they could draw upon from the Ingleby report to match Kilbrandon in boldness. It must have been trying for Sir Charles Cunningham, Permanent Secretary of the Home Office, to be upstaged by his former colleagues at the Scottish Office.

Such was the strength of the opposition that the white paper was quietly withdrawn, and by 1966 a new Home Secretary, Roy Jenkins, was encouraging his officials to begin thinking afresh. In August 1966 Derek Morell joined the Children's Department, and it was agreed that legislation on young offenders would be attended to. A way forward would be found that did not mimic Scotland or incite the full wrath of the Magistrates' Association. Morrell and Joan Cooper, recently appointed as Chief Inspector of the Children's Department, had *Children in Trouble* ready in early 1968. The second white paper, which did not deal with young adults, proposed that the juvenile court be retained. The recommendation was sufficient to keep the Magistrates' Association at bay, which, under moderate leadership, expressed more muted criticism than three years earlier.

The white paper and the subsequent Children and Young Persons Act 1969 sought to blur the categories of juveniles before the court. It was the government's intention sequentially to increase the age of criminal responsibility to fourteen. Care rather than criminal proceedings was to be preferred. Courts were no longer able to make an approved-school order but instead might consider making a care or supervision order to the local authority. It was at this point that the welfare approach found its clearest expression, with considerable discretionary powers entrusted to social workers regarding placements within the care order, regardless of the reason for the order having been made. This might include placement in a 'community home with education on the premises', formerly approved schools. A sequential strategy was also employed in the legislation with reference to the removal of all juveniles from the prison system. It was intended that detention centres and borstals for juveniles would be phased out as alternative resources became available, including those implied by 'Intermediate Treatment'.* This was less a policy of decarceration than a reiteration of the traditional welfare abhorrence of the prison system. In fact the 1969 Act and the preceding discussions and debates failed to address directly the issue of institutions. The distinction was not between institutions and alternatives but between treatment/welfare (which might include institutions) and punishment (which included sanctions such as attendance centres). While supporters of the Act sought to end the use of the prison system, regarded as punitive, there was no objection to institutions tied to the care system. Indeed, the white paper stated: 'These proposals will not diminish the need for residential facilities. In particular, the retention of the seventeenth birthday as the upper age limit for the juvenile courts means that all the existing approved schools, including the senior schools, will probably be required for the accommodation of children and young persons in care.' Furthermore, plans had been under way since 1967 to establish two or three youth treatment centres to be administered by central government. These facilities were to be 'therapeutic communities', and the admission of children in care was to be made not by courts but by social workers.

The welfare and treatment reformers of the late 1960s were retreading the path of Mary Carpenter and Mathew Davenport Hill of 120 years before. It was not all institutions, but the prison system's institutions, which were bad for young people. The

---

* The legislation was steered through the House of Commons by James Callaghan, who had become Home Secretary in November 1967. Speaking at a conference in 1968 he spoke of young people 'going through the difficult phase of obsolescence'.

way forward lay in improved management, staff recruitment and training, and more sophisticated institutional treatment methods. The notion of the therapeutic community, which a decade earlier received little support in England, now took hold in the planning of the new-look institutions, serving also as a rationale for locking up young people and masking realities of institutional life. For example, the general view emerging from a conference of professionals held in 1968 was that much longer periods in institutions were required than the average stay of about eighteen months (Sparks and Hood, 1968, p. 10). The director of the first youth treatment centre declared: 'Treatment is the total living situation, all the waking hours of the young person and particularly those immediately before he goes to sleep, when he is warm, comfortable and surrounded by those adults with whom he has warm and secure relationships' (Edwards, 1976, p. 9).

Considerable optimism was expressed by proponents of the treatment idea. Given well-trained staff the technology was available to bring about the required changes in young people. It was not until the early seventies that this euphoria was dampened by a close reading of the evaluative research and by concerns as to legal protection of young people from the excesses of treatment and welfare.

The movement of the 1960s was one of ideas more than practice. Treatment and welfare were heralded as the ways forward, but the apparatus was never in place for these themes to be implemented fully. Despite declarations that a new dawn was imminent, the punishment approach was far from dormant. In 1964 the first of several secure units was opened which, after 1969, were the responsibility of departments of social services.* By the end of the decade the

---

* By 1981 there were 450 secure places at the local level of government (including the two youth treatment centres) and a further 150 places under construction. The daily cost per child at one London secure unit, as of March 1984, was £164 (Orchard Lodge Regional Resource Centre).

national detention centre network was in place, coinciding with the new statute which promised that detention centre sentences for juveniles be phased out. But it was the ideas and attitudes of the sixties, culminating in the 1969 Act, rather than any real shift in practice on which the campaign for counter-reform was to be mounted.

Punishment rules

The contours of the campaign to strengthen further the sentencing powers of the courts can most clearly be discerned with respect to juvenile offenders. Commencing in the early 1970s, howls of protest erupted from the Magistrates' Association. At the Association's annual meeting in October 1972, a resolution calling for a review of the Act was agreed upon. The proposer, Mrs Rose of Hertfordshire, declared: 'The youngsters were learning to laugh at, and to flaunt authority and to treat the law with contempt, and this was not helping them to take their place in society.' Also passed without dissent was a resolution that priority be given for more detention centres in the prison-building programme. The chairman of the Juvenile Courts Committee, Mr R. C. Stranger, argued that detention centres 'were intended to halt anti-social behaviour through early recognition and adequate treatment before the offender became institutionalized. They ought to be complementary to intermediate treatment, not an alternative.' Seconding the resolution, Lady Burman deplored the absence of detention centre vacancies which she claimed had occurred on at least 2,000 occasions the previous year. Again imagery of the taunting youngster was invoked: 'When a young thug came into court with a grin on his face it was very salutary that he should leave that court immediately in a police van for an institution where he would have a spell of discipline.' Another resolution, carried on a majority of voices, called for more borstals and for magistrates to be able to sentence directly without committal to the Crown Court.

In January 1973 the Magistrates' Association convened a national conference on the Act, attended by 350 chairmen and deputy chairmen of juvenile benches and representatives from social services, probation and other organizations. Sir Keith Joseph, then Secretary of State for Social Services, told the conference: 'You have many, many very legitimate worries and complaints. Please don't spoil your admirable record of public service by, in any part of the country, making it more difficult for the social services departments to consult with you, to explain to you, and to co-ordinate with you, when they seek to do so.' Joseph pointed out that detention centres and borstals remained available for juveniles and that there were plans for a substantial increase in secure places at the local level. Joseph refused to repeal the Act but, behind the scenes, the campaign to strengthen the powers of the courts was being carried forward. In December 1973 the Expenditure Committee of the House of Commons decided to examine the workings of the Act. The Committee's inquiry was delayed as Parliament was dissolved for the February election of 1974 which brought Labour back to power. The Conservative manifesto promised to review and amend the 1969 Act. A glimpse of attitudes within the Labour Government is provided by Barbara Castle, who noted in her diary that some senior members of the cabinet were by no means unsympathetic to the Conservative position. Describing the joint meeting between the cabinet and the National Executive Committee on the manifesto she writes:

Things sobered up as we turned to the section on the rights of the individual and my never very dormant affection for Roy [Jenkins] lit up again as I heard him say, 'I am against entering into a law and order auction' . . . Jim [Callaghan] came out in typical colours: 'I agree, but I am rather in favour of dealing with teenage hooliganism' adding that he greatly admired the section on this in the Tory

Manifesto and wished he had anything as good as this in ours. Dennis [Healey]: 'Hear, Hear.' (Castle, 1980, pp. 181–2)

In July the Expenditure Committee resumed work only to be delayed again by a second dissolution of Parliament. In the same month the legal affairs correspondent of *The Times* claimed there was 'virtually a juvenile crime wave' and recited horror stories arising from the inadequate powers of the juvenile courts. His book ended: 'Our society must reconcile itself to the idea that it is going to lock up more children in the future than in the recent past. We believe this is the only possible way to help deal with the growing problem of juvenile crime and to help the juvenile criminals themselves' (Berlins and Wansell, 1974, p. 124). The pressure was maintained during the period the committee took evidence. Early in 1975 a deputation from the Magistrates' Association met with the Home Secretary and the Secretary of State for Social Services. At this meeting the Magistrates' Association emphasized the importance it attached to maintaining both junior and senior detention centres: 'Our leaders came away feeling that they had had a full and fair – and indeed sympathetic – hearing. Beyond doubt, measures are on the way to make substantial improvements in the working of the Act, both to safeguard society and to deal more effectively with the tough minority of persistent juvenile offenders.'

In evidence to the committee, the Magistrates' Association referred to 'a minority of tough sophisticated young criminals ... [who] ... prey on the community, at will, even after the courts have placed them in care. They deride the powerlessness of the courts to do anything effective.' Sir William Addison talked of 'the hard core of young offenders – that is to say, the offenders in the youngest age group – that is now resulting in the very serious increase in the incidence of crime in the 15 to 17 year old groups.' Mr R. C. Stranger added: 'The hard core of sophisticated young criminals hitherto considered and spoken of as small in number but which one fears [is] increasing' (Expenditure Committee, Vol. 2, 1975, pp. 128–31).

The Magistrates' Association's case for institutions was based largely on the 'hard-core' notion: 'The essential problem is [therefore] to provide the courts with greater powers and facilities where they are clearly needed for persistent young offenders.' Other groups, in evidence to the Committee, side-stepped the question of institutions. Only NACRO (National Association for the Care and Resettlement of Offenders) specifically urged the phasing out of detention centres and borstals. The committee's report, published in July 1975, represented a striking achievement for the Magistrates' Association. The recommendations largely reflected the ambiguity and lack of clearly defined objectives which characterized much of the evidence. In their final paragraph the committee stated: 'We strongly recommend, within the framework of the Act, a major shift of emphasis away from custodial and punitive techniques and towards intermediate schemes, supervision, and a much greater use of non-residential care, especially fostering' (Expenditure Committee, Vol. 1, 1975, p. xlix). But the committee blunted the force of this language by recommending that secure accommodation at the local level be increased, that courts be enabled to impose secure care orders, and that the minimum length of sentences to detention centres be reduced to two days. The Expenditure Committee rejected NACRO's argument that detention centres and borstals be replaced by the 200 beds planned for youth treatment centres, commenting: 'A considerable change in the attitude of magistrates, and of society as a whole, to the containment of delinquent youngsters would be necessary before such a total number of secure places could suffice' (Expenditure Committee, Vol. 1, 1975, p. xlx).

At the annual meeting of the Magistrates' Association in October 1975, reference was made to the achievements 'made in the face of government activity'. The meeting went on to carry unanimously a further broadside on the Act as an attempt to gain government support for the Expenditure Committee's recommendations. One speaker offered the view that 'total breakdown could not be far away'. However, in May 1976, the Government rejected both secure care orders and shorter detention centre orders and, instead, encouraged consultative arrangements between the various parties at the local level. The Magistrates' Association found the Government's response to be 'disappointing and inadequate in failing to give juvenile courts the powers they needed'.

It was not until 1977 that a strategy of decarceration was spelled out. After considering evidence on the Massachusetts experience, a NACRO committee, under Peter Jay, suggested that a total of 400 secure places were required for juveniles in England and Wales and recommended that no other institutional provision be made (Jay, 1977, pp. 49–54). Two years later a similar stance was taken to the situation in Northern Ireland by the Black committee, which recommended that secure capacity be limited to 120 places and that other institutions be closed (Black, 1979, pp. 48–9).

Practice and policy with respect to young adults and crime remained firmly tied to the prison system. The legislation of 1969 did not deal with young adults, and in 1970 the Advisory Council on the Penal System was asked to undertake a major review. Four years later, under Sir Kenneth Younger, the committee called for action 'to effect a major shift of emphasis from treatment in custody to the control, support and care of the offender in the community' (Younger, 1974, p. v). In particular, Younger recommended a control and supervision order which would give the probation service enhanced discretionary powers over young adults in the community. Many probation officers were unhappy about becoming 'screws on wheels', and some academic commentators were concerned about the considerable discretionary decision-making left to both the prison and probation authorities and regretted Younger's apparent indifference to the emerging justice model. The consequence of these and other objections to Younger was drift and inertia, which encouraged the Home Office to side-step Younger's central issue, namely shifting resources from custody to supporting young adults in the community.

It is worth noting that both the Younger and Ingleby committees deliberated for four years, in contrast to the one year taken by the equally thorough work of the Gladstone and Lushington committees in the 1890s. It seems likely that in the case of the Younger committee some of the impetus for action was lost by the delay in producing the report. A further four years elapsed before the Labour government produced a green paper in December 1978, but this document, an initiative taken within the prison system, was entirely devoted to streamlining custodial arrangements. After the Conservative election victory, events moved rapidly. The Conservative manifesto of 1979 had promised to strengthen sentencing powers with respect to juveniles and young adults and, fifteen months later, the Government published a white paper, *Young Offenders*.* The warm reception given it by the Magistrates' Association was hardly surprising, as the white paper met most of its demands of the previous fifteen years. The proposals formed the basis of the Criminal Justice Act 1982, which took effect in 1983. Ivan Lawrence QC, MP welcomed the legislation: 'One of the most important steps in the bill which I strongly welcome is the reflection of public opinion which says that we are fed up with letting sentences

---

* The principal authors were Leon Brittan, then Minister of State at the Home Office, and Roger Sims (formerly on the Council of the Magistrates' Association), Parliamentary Private Secretary to William Whitelaw, the Home Secretary.

be decided by social workers rather than the courts ...
encouraged by wet socialist intellectuals from all over the
place.'

The Criminal Justice Act 1982 performed the *coup de grâce*
for borstals. Sentences of youth custody, fixed in length by
the courts, replaced borstal and prison sentences for persons
aged under twenty-one. Borstal staff were returned to uniform after having been in civilian clothes for sixty years. The
'penal reformatory' experiment, launched by the Gladstone
committee in 1895, was over. The white paper had promised
to retain 'the best of borstal' but youth custody is much closer
in concept to the Parkhurst of the 1940s than to the innovative
years between the wars. The overt confirmation of the
punishment approach was even more apparent with the new
focus on detention centres. In 1970 the Advisory Council on
the Penal System had recommended that loss of liberty be
the only punitive element to detention centres. Steps were
taken during the 1970s to humanize the regimes, but these
ended at the Conservative Party annual conference of 1979.
William Whitelaw, then Home Secretary, announced that an
experimental tougher regime in two centres would be evalu-
ated. The result of the study by prison system psychologists
was finally published in the early summer of 1984. No
discernible difference was found in outcome between the
experimental and the other detention centres which were
studied. Despite the study's findings Leon Brittan, the new
Home Secretary, announced that aspects of the 'tougher
regime' (increased emphasis on parades and inspections,
demanding work, fewer privileges and a brisker tempo)
would be extended to all detention centres. A vignette of the
detention centre at Send provides a picture of how 14–16
year olds are received from the court:

The boy is hurried from the [police] car into the building, moving
very fast. An officer stands very close to him and shouts commands.

The officers behave like stereotyped sergeant majors because they are convinced of the value of setting the tone of the place at the start. They believe that a strict reception and induction procedure is an essential control mechanism for an institution that has a high turnover of trainees. There is rarely personal animosity towards a particular trainee. Instead officers tend to have a somewhat jaundiced view of the whole class. (Home Office, 1984a, p. 82)

By the mid-1980s the punishment approach was supreme. The only deliberately punitive institutions within the prison system were exclusively for its youngest inmates.

Tis has an uphill struggle

Chapter Three

A Quantum Leap

In terms of ideology, the question of correctional reform is not whether we can break out of previous definitions to more up-to-date definitions. It is whether we can effectively break the vicious circle of definitions calling for institutional arrangements which, in turn, revalidate the definitions; and build into new definitions, since they will come, enough categories that show the social and psychological strengths and lifespan of those defined as delinquent or criminal. (Jerome Miller, 1973, p. 6)

A clue to your philosophy is your blithe description of delinquents as 'kids'. Many of the 'kids' I see every day in juvenile court are sexually precocious, street wise and sadistic. You may think they can be absorbed into decent society without discipline but I don't. And if I were you I wouldn't be too hard on the judge who sent a 'kid' to Camp Hill for knocking over tombstones. Any 'kid' who would destroy a gravemarker is capable of pushing his mother off a ninety foot cliff. (Letter from a juvenile court judge to Dr Jerome Miller, Commissioner of the Office of Children and Youth, Pennsylvania, 1975)

•

In the early months of 1972 the state of Massachusetts drew widespread attention with the abrupt closure of its 'training schools', incarcerative institutions holding young offenders. Jerry Miller, as head of the Department of Youth Services, pursued a 'deep end' strategy in seeking juvenile justice

Unattributed quotations in this chapter are from the BBC radio documentary *The Massachusetts Alternative*, first broadcast on 2 May 1984.

reform by greatly reducing institutional capacity *prior* to setting up community-based alternatives. Miller was convinced that the alternative and more conventional 'shallow end' strategy, of first developing alternatives and later phasing out institutions, would widen the net, with institutions remaining alongside new community-based programmes.

In 1969 facilities for juvenile offenders in Massachusetts were not very different from those existing today in much of the United States and Western Europe. Most young people on remand for the courts were held in secure detention centres, and those who had been sentenced were located in rurally isolated institutions known as training schools, some of which dated from the 1840s, including the Lyman school which was favourably commented upon by Mary Carpenter in 1853. Despite pretensions that these institutions provided treatment, they had in recent years become severely discredited.

The political conditions for change in Massachusetts were generally favourable. Throughout the 1960s the Division for Youth Services had been subjected to fierce criticism. State and federal inquiries had reported widescale abuses and recommended major changes. These demands for reform were supported by many sections of the media, in particular the influential *Boston Globe*. In January 1969 Francis Sargent, a liberal Republican, became governor and within two months had secured the resignation of the long-term head of the Division for Youth Services. In August, legislation which had been stalled in previous years was enacted, creating a new organizational structure with considerable authority and discretionary powers invested in the commissioner. Sargent appointed a selection committee to undertake a nationwide search for a commissioner. After considering some fifty applicants, the committee recommended that the governor appoint Dr Jerome Miller. Miller became the first commissioner of the newly constituted Department of Youth Services in October 1969.

Jerry Miller was born and raised in Fergus Falls, a rural community in north-eastern Minnesota. At the age of eighteen he entered Maryknoll Seminary and for the next five years underwent training for the priesthood. On leaving the order, where he gained a master's degree in social work, he was drafted into the United States Air Force and for ten years was an officer social worker dealing mainly with the children of air force personnel. During five years in England, based at Lakenheath, he was impressed by Maxwell Jones's pioneering work on the therapeutic community and with residential settings created by George Lyward and Ronald Laing. On leaving the air force in 1968, he returned to the United States and, after a very brief spell with the Department of Youth Services in Maryland, he joined the Faculty of Social Work at Ohio State University. Miller has described the institutions as he found them on arrival in Massachusetts:

The stress was on security and discipline. In fact the superintendent of one facility told me that it was his job to break kids down; that's how you change people – you break them down to nothing. They were really highly supervised: most of the doors were locked when the kids went in and out, they were watched with staff who followed them around with two-way radios. For instance, at Shirley, whenever they marched from cottage to cottage, you would see a staff person, usually in a very large car, driving behind all these kids as they walked in a row.

And at the Lancaster girls' training school Miller found that the girls

wore long house dresses, or smocks that went almost to the floor. They were allowed no make-up, they were only allowed one bath a week, they had to sit in silence, and the only game allowed was Jacks ... they'd sit around and bounce little balls. Every girl was

69

given a vaginal exam as a routine, which was just barbaric. It was just a horrific, repressive and awful place.

A former inmate of Shirley Industrial School, Michael Radan, subsequently the director of a hostel for young offenders, has described the consequences of absconding:

If you tried to escape they usually had what they called goon squads. Staff members would go off and they would pick up usually the biggest and brawniest kids – and in most cases they were black – give them bats, put them in the back of the jeep, and they went looking for you. If they found you, you got a good whipping, and then brought back into discipline. I had seen kids come back with very severely bruised ... broken bones; and that was a time for other inmates to really beat the hell out of you.

During his first year as commissioner, Miller's principal goal was to humanize the training schools and to incorporate methods from the notion of the therapeutic community. He was sharply critical of existing arrangements, believing it was necessary to rebuke publicly his own department and, by implication, many of its personnel. Miller capitalized upon the groundswell for reform across the state, and actively encouraged the media to dramatically portray the institutions as destructive places. He regularly took part in television and radio shows and spoke at meetings throughout the state. On some of these occasions he brought along young people who persuasively echoed his dismay at the existing institutional conditions. Miller's purpose was also to change the widely held impression that young people involved in crime are of vicious and alarming appearance. He later commented:

I think we found many natural allies, surprisingly perhaps from the more conservative end of the spectrum. I knew when the chips were down in Massachusetts, particularly during a couple of critical periods, that I could depend much better on the people toward the conservative end of the spectrum such as Lions Clubs, Kywanis and Rotary, than I could on my more natural liberal allies.

Miller gained early support from the leadership of the state legislature, and although he had a number of persistent political enemies he sometimes encouraged such opposition to polarize issues so as to encourage support from persons who had been previously undecided. In what became a moral crusade for children in trouble, he had the backing of a variety of groups, from the League of Women Voters to the Lifers' Group at Walpole Prison. These and other non-professional groups were consistently more supportive to Miller than social workers and persons associated with established prison reform groups, many of whom remained uncertain of the implications for them.

Miller and his colleagues set about the uphill task of attempting to make the institutions into decent places. His first obstacle was to get institutional staff even to acknowledge what was going on. He has described the difficulties:

I confronted the superintendent and assistant superintendent about the conditions in the facility and said that I wanted them to do away with the silence rule immediately, and to get a television and books in there at least so there would be something going on. I was told there was no silence rule; the boys just didn't wish to talk. It took us the better part of four meetings with the superintendent to establish that in fact there was a silence rule in that cottage, and we established it by accident. They were concerned I was going to close the cottage, which I eventually did, and in order to justify it after our first meeting they circulated a pseudo-sociological questionnaire to all the boys: 'I like Cottage 9 because . . .' with three choices. One of the questions on the second page was: 'I think the silence rule is a good idea.' Then I had them, because the administration had admitted in their own writing that there was a silence rule.

Attempts were made to train personnel in treatment techniques and to provide them with a broader understanding of the needs of young people. These efforts included sessions in group techniques and the therapeutic community. Among the training consultants at one session was Maxwell Jones, whom Miller had met some years before in Britain. Miller became increasingly aware of the difficulties in improving the quality of personnel and disillusioned about the prospect for sustained institutional change. He later described an occasion when Maxwell Jones was brought into one of the institutions:

We're in the midst of these sharing therapeutic group encounters where all the staff and all the youngsters are having this large Maxwell Jones type meeting, and in the midst of it the superintend-ent calls a line-up, and all the boys had to leave and go outside and stand in a line and be counted. Of course, they responded then by one of them running away and stealing a staff person's car during the conference, resulting in all sorts of people running in all directions to chase him. I can recall Maxwell Jones, as he left, pulling me aside and saying perhaps with this group his ideas might not work, and what he meant by the group were not the boys but the staff. He was simply not used to that kind of community meeting.

A number of considerations began to convince Miller that more radical measures might have to be taken. The institu-tional staff remained hostile to the reform initiatives, and there were even occasions when some staff attempted to discredit what Miller was doing by encouraging runaways. Furthermore, it required enormous effort and endurance to maintain the momentum for change, and Miller became increasingly struck by the tendency of institutions to slide back to a deadening routine. Miller was aware that institu-tions 'cannot sustain their decency over an extended period of time. They tend ultimately to move toward repression and violence at worst, and apathy at best. And apathy is ultimately violence'. Miller also recognized the ease with which a future commissioner would be able to undo any progress, and that humanization of the institutions, at best, could provide little more than short-term relief. Finally, Miller and his colleagues became impressed with the possibilities of extending the group therapy techniques into community settings far removed from the context of the incarcerative institution.

The process of youth decarceration in Massachusetts did not emerge from a preconceived plan but was the culmination of a series of events or, to use Miller's word, 'accidents'. The first institution to be closed was the maximum-security facility located at Bridgewater Correctional Institution, the state facility for the criminally insane, jointly administered by the departments of corrections and mental health and the setting for the celebrated Fred Wiseman documentary film *Titicut Follies*. Miller was appalled by the conditions at this eighty-bed unit, designated the Institute for Juvenile Guidance. On one occasion he visited the institution with Jessie Sargent, wife of the state governor. Miller takes up the story:

It was common to see kids there spread-eagled, handcuffed to their beds and that sort of thing, and staff always justified it by saying these were the worst of the worst, the most difficult. As we went into the main building there were no youngsters ... it was quite silent, and there was a smell of urine, and water around on the floors. It was a foul old institution. And as we walked into the yard there was a commotion in the middle of the yard and suddenly a number of kids ran for the walls, in different directions, staff were running and pulling them down ... and handcuffing them, and beating and swearing at them. Then the kids began to punch out windows and we had the beginnings of a little riot. Then the staff individually went in and got kids and put them in their cells and they were very roughly handled and I remember Mrs Sargent being very taken aback at that. She went around room to room, or cell to cell, talking to the youngsters through the little holes. As we were walking out she said to me, 'how can these kids get any better working with people like this', meaning the staff. I would guess for the governor's wife, it was one of the more exciting evenings of her career, and I thought she's probably going to whisper something in the governor's ear about this. So we decided this was our opportunity to close it, and we transferred maybe a dozen or fifteen to another institution, and we paroled the rest. At that time, probably it was my own naïvety about government, but I don't recall ever asking the governor . . . I don't even think I told him.

The institution at Bridgewater was closed in October 1970. By first closing the most secure of the system's institutions, holding supposedly the most difficult young people, Miller had begun the process of decarceration at the deep end.

During his early months in office Miller was able to make overall reductions in the training school populations by reducing the length of stay. As commissioner he had authority to parole young people and to transfer them to alternative programmes. He did not have the authority actually to close the institutions or to dismiss personnel. Miller's own account illustrates his opportunistic tactics:

I sent out a memo really to protect myself politically, in which I said, or I thought I said, every youngster will have to do at least three months with us before he can be considered for return. My own ambivalence about the memo must have come through, or the staff wishing to see me in a certain way or perhaps even wishing to set me up a bit, interpreted the memo to mean no youngster may do more than three months, that they have to be sent home within three months. I got a call from a judge one day, not a terribly friendly judge, who was very upset about a youngster that had been sent home and he said he'd only been there a matter of three or four weeks; and I said well that's impossible, I sent out a memo saying he had to stay there, and as I recall the amount of time was three months, it may have been six, but I think it was three months. And I called the institution to check and he said, 'Oh sure, we're going along with your memo, everybody has to be sent home within three months of their commitment.' And lo and behold they'd been sending all these kids home early . . . by mistake really. Well then I thought about it, and I said my gosh, I've only gotten one call from one judge who's not friendly anyway . . . and they'd been going home . . . by the dozens and nobody seems upset, and nothing's happening. So I said let's keep our mouths shut, and I didn't call the judge back or anything, and I just didn't say anything about it, and the population just fell precipitously because they were sending everybody home, and no one was making a to-do about it. It was our chance because we were moving in that direction anyway, but that's how we lowered that population so dramatically – by accident.

Miller displayed considerable ingenuity in side-stepping bureaucratic obstacles. For example, although he was not able to dismiss training school superintendents, he was authorized to grant leaves of absence. By persuading the superintendent of Shirley Industrial School to take sick leave the *de facto* control of the school was placed with one of his key aides, Paul de Muro, who once taught medieval English literature at Ohio State University, and who had been appointed to the one vacant staff position, as janitor to the institution. By speeding up the parole processes de Muro attempted during 1971 to phase out the Shirley school population, but his efforts were continually thwarted by staff resistance. By the end of the year Miller decided that gradual decarceration was far from inevitable:

I felt that if we could show that we could deal with the most 'dangerous' kids in the department, supposedly, and I say that in quotes because they really weren't but they were defined that way ... If we could deal with them in other ways than this kind of locked institution ... well then one automatically would deal decently – hopefully – with simple burglars or runaways or whatever. We really thought that we were quite expendable at that time, that the idea the staff had was that 'commissioners come and go but we'll be here forever, and let's just ride him out, let's go through whatever routine we have to to convince him that we've changed our ways, but he'll soon leave and then we can go back to business as usual', so that we decided to pretend we were expendable, and that we would be replaced by Heinrich Himmler and the SS. Given that, how do you design a system that would make it difficult for Heinrich to make the system brutal? Well the first thing you do is to close the institutions and scatter the youngsters in all directions to various programmes.

Miller became confident that it would be politically feasible abruptly to transfer the young people remaining in the training schools to alternative programmes. The main effort to transfer young people from the training schools took place in January 1972, through a novel and effective device. About a hundred young people (including some girls from the Lancaster institution) participated in a one-month residential conference on deinstitutionalization held on the campus of the University of Massachusetts at Amherst in the western part of the state. Joint student/youth groups had the goal of developing alternative placement plans for the young people so that it would not be necessary for them to return to the training schools. The 'conference' was run in a rather informal manner, with one research team commenting: 'Advocates and "their kids" did their own thing and for the most part this appeared to work out rather well' (Coates, Miller and Ohlin, 1973). The conference was timed to coincide with university holidays, and it also occurred at a time when the state legislature was not in session. The day before the conference one of Miller's assistants briefed a senior aide of the governor as to what had been planned, and it was arranged that the governor should visit Amherst to participate in part of the proceedings. The final training school to be closed was the Lancaster School for Girls, abandoned in 1975. The fact that the institution for girls was the most difficult to close reflected both the department's neglect of the need to develop alternative placements for girls and strong resistance to efforts to phase out the institution.

Instead of incarcerative institutions, Miller and his colleagues sought access to a wide variety of programmes which would meet the diverse needs of young people. He was convinced that most of these programmes should be purchased from community groups and private non-profit agencies rather than being directly provided by the department. Traditional welfare agencies such as the New England Home for Little Wanderers were among the new vendors, as were projects run by ex-prisoners and an array of treatment programmes. For the most part, the programmes did not exist prior to the removal of the young people from the institutions. The new alternatives to incarceration sprang up in a necessarily haphazard and uneven fashion, and some observers have described those times as being chaotic.

During the final months of Miller's period as commissioner severe strains were placed on the state's bureaucratic processes. The fundamental problem was that the department was still paying the salaries of institutional staff and for the upkeep of empty buildings in addition to paying the increasing number of private agencies which provided the new programmes. By forcing the bureaucracy to adapt painfully to the new situation, Miller overcame one of the most formidable obstacles to decarceration. In January 1973, Miller left Massachusetts to become director of the Illinois Department of Children and Family Services, where he remained as director until August 1974. Joe Leavey, Miller's deputy, became acting commissioner. Leavey was from south Boston and, prior to joining Youth Services, he had been with the Department of Welfare. Miller was convinced that Leavey would be in a better position to bring about the needed bureaucratic adaptations and to reach agreement with the various interest groups, such as the juvenile court judges, many of whom remained opposed to the changes. During his two years as commissioner, Leavey made some progress in consolidating the new arrangements, giving particular attention to problems associated with the provision of secure placements. Much of his energy, however, was absorbed in dealing with attacks on the department's credibility and effectiveness. Leavey's position was also weakened by the failure of the new Democratic governor, Michael Dukakis, to seek his confirmation as commissioner.

During the latter part of 1975 the Department of Youth

Services was subjected to a barrage of criticism from the media. The most concerted of these attacks was launched by a Boston television station during September. In a series of editorials, aired several times a day over a two-week period, calls were made for Leavey's resignation. Much of the criticism centred on the question of secure facilities for serious juvenile offenders. The last of these editorials demanded that Leavey be fired and that the number of secure beds be increased, commenting: 'A great deal of today's violent crime is committed by juveniles. Massachusetts simply cannot afford a Department of Youth Services which is so demonstrably incompetent.' In response to the criticism Leavey stated: 'We are attempting to establish small secure units that will provide security and treatment, yet will not repeat the abuses of jail-like settings.' The pressure on Leavey intensified and he resigned in December 1975.

Leavey was followed as commissioner by Jack Calhoun, then director of the Justice Resource Institute in Boston, an agency responsible for a variety of experimental programmes in criminal justice. In his first twelve months Calhoun was determined to speed up the process of consolidation. In particular, he stressed the need for administrative and programmatic standards and the capacity to monitor the quality of services provided for young people.

The period 1973–8 under Leavey and Calhoun was primarily characterized by attempts to consolidate DYS's new role. Both commissioners focused on programme development and on overcoming the polarized public perceptions of youth correction, distrust by the legislature, and severe fiscal and management problems. Calhoun was especially concerned with the establishment of standards and the quality control of programmes. Both commissioners were subject to considerable political pressures, especially in their relationships with the courts. The overriding issue during this period was the number of secure beds available for young people committed to the department. Calhoun's response to the secure beds question was to establish a task force under Scott Harshbarger, then an assistant state attorney-general, to consider what was required. In 1977, Harshbarger recommended a slight increase in secure bed provision, taking some of the political pressure off the department (Harshbarger, 1977). However, in 1978 Massachusetts voters elected Edward King as governor. King, a right-wing Democrat, had defeated the liberal Democrat Michael Dukakis on a bold law-and-order manifesto. Seven months later Calhoun resigned.

When Edward King was sworn in as governor it seemed probable that over the next four years the decarceration process would be reversed. It was expected that King's choice for commissioner would share his highly conservative views on criminal justice. Alarming to the advocates of decarceration was the prospect of a successful legislative bid to provide the judiciary with direct sentencing powers. Bills incorporating direct sentencing provisions had been introduced on a regular basis since the closure of the institutions, but each failed to get sufficient legislative support. To the surprise of close observers of the Massachusetts scene none of these fears materialized.

The Appointment of Edward Murphy as Commissioner

Edward Murphy was appointed to head the department in October 1979. Before taking up the position, an earlier nominee of the governor's had left to take an appointment in another state. One observer commented that 'some early King appointments had exploded' and that King primarily sought a politically neutral but effective administrator. Murphy's background was in the federal probation and parole service, and at the time of his appointment he was responsible for central and western Massachusetts. He was experienced in community-based programmes but was new to juvenile justice. Murphy's appointment prompted a negative comment in the *Boston Globe* but little was known of his views. Murphy has recalled that his mandate from the governor's office was 'absence of pain'.

The question of returning to the use of training schools never arose in Murphy's discussions with the governor or with Murphy's immediate superior, the Secretary for Human Services. Indeed, Secretary Mahoney, who in the late 1960s had been an attorney in a case involving the Bridgewater Institute for Juvenile Guidance which revealed gross institutional conditions, certainly had no wish to turn back the clock. The central issue then, as before, was the number of secure beds. At the news conference announcing his appointment, Murphy was asked how many secure beds were required. An off-the-cuff response of 'maybe two hundred' was interpreted by the media as a substantial increase. Murphy later said he did not regret this reply as he thought his department gained support from criminal justice and other groups.

Edward Murphy's initial perception of the department was that 'some very severe management problems' existed. He was determined to put these right and to improve the department's image: 'We needed to convince the public we knew what we were doing.' Murphy brought in several professionals from outside Massachusetts. One of these was his deputy, Edward Loughran, who had been with the New York State Division for Youth for nine years and who was glad to get away from an increasingly repressive scene. The cover of the department's annual report for 1982 carried a quotation from Alfred North Whitehead: 'The art of progress is to preserve order amid change and to preserve change amid order.' A senior civil servant put it another way:

'Edward Murphy represented stability . . . we had come close to losing the whole ball of wax.'

Murphy maintains that the threat to deinstitutionalization came less from the King administration than from the legislature. In particular, he had in mind a bill to enable judges to decide upon secure placements of young people sentenced to the department. Strengthening the powers of the courts in this way was strongly endorsed by a committee set up by the governor, which allowed for secure orders of up to six months for repeat-offenders and of up to twelve months for serious-injury cases.* In 1983 the bill was approved by the House but failed to get through the Senate. Democratic representative Paul White, a conservative on law-and-order issues, declared: 'The real negative of DYS is the complete inability of judges to deal with the juvenile hard core.' Powerful opposition in the Senate, including the chairman of the Ways and Means Committee, blocked the bill. The chairman of the Senate Committee on Criminal Justice held that 'DYS has the expertise'.

'Despite the efforts of the King administration, in reality they were not able to achieve much.' So concluded Yitzhak Bakal, an assistant commissioner under Jerry Miller and later head of the Northeastern Family Institute, a major vendor with DYS. Similarly Susan Wayne, another former assistant commissioner under Jack Calhoun and later executive director of another large vendor, Justice Resource Institute, would not have predicted that DYS would emerge unscathed. In January 1983 Edward King was replaced as governor with the re-election of Michael Dukakis. There was general approval when Dukakis retained Edward Murphy as commissioner. Murphy represented predictability, credibility and

* Governor King established his Task Force on Juvenile Crime in October 1980 under the chairmanship of Judge James Nixon. The Task Force, which included Judge Poitrast of Boston Juvenile Court, Commissioner Murphy and James Q. Wilson of Harvard, reported in April 1981.

stability. During 1982 Murphy described how his role differed from Miller's: 'The task facing juvenile justice administrators in Massachusetts is to institutionalize the positive aspects of the change that had occurred here. The success of this goal does not depend on charismatic leadership and artful polemics. It depends instead on the development of consensus and the creation of a lasting infrastructure organized around the basic principles that our professional experience has taught us.'* Murphy was a pragmatic manager rather than a crusader and a commissioner who saw his department as a correctional agency; Miller saw his task as changing society's perception of young people involved in crime.

Indications of Slippage

Towards the end of Edward King's administration, a leading child advocacy group published a highly critical report on remand practice in Massachusetts.† In September 1983 Jerry Miller published an article in the *Boston Globe* headed 'DYS – Back to Bad Old Days', which, while critical in tone, was probably intended as a warning shot. Interviewed some months later, Miller's assessment was that developments in Massachusetts were holding up quite well.

Slippage from the decarceration process is explored with reference to the following considerations: the number of secure treatment beds; detention practice; transfers to adult

---

* Remarks at a conference held at the University of Massachusetts at Amherst on 8 January 1982, to mark the tenth anniversary of the closing of the Lyman School for Boys.

† Massachusetts Advocacy Center, *Delinquent Justice. Juvenile Detention Practice in Massachusetts*, Boston, 1980. The report concluded: 'The youth services revolution in Massachusetts has not failed, but it remains unfinished.'

courts; the development of the network of community-based programmes; and the strength of groups supporting decarceration.

The number of secure 'treatment' beds

The most volatile issue has continued to be the provision of secure settings for certain groups of juveniles, especially those sentenced for the most serious offences. The development of a wide variety of programmes in the community has demonstrated that these are appropriate even for some juveniles involved in serious offences. Non-residential programmes, such as 'tracking', can provide a high level of surveillance, where very regular contact is maintained between streetworkers and young people.

The threat to decarceration in Massachusetts is not a return to large institutions but to a substantial increase in secure beds. Establishing the optimum level of secure beds while maintaining the decarceration process involves a host of political and programmatic considerations. Miller's position was that the number of secure beds should be kept very low, and that the ceiling be tightly enforced: regional offices were given quotas, and an additional placement meant someone had to be removed from the secure setting. Miller saw 'dangerousness' as being defined by continual political negotiation, and without vigilance the definition would broaden. On the other hand, there is a widely held opinion that, should the number of secure beds become too small, the decarceration process would be placed in jeopardy. For example, Edward Murphy regards the provision of additional secure beds as essential to gain the credibility that makes the department politically viable.

The issues surrounding the provision of secure beds have been clouded by ambiguity and confusion. Two problems arise. First, security is achieved by some programmes through

83

high staff numbers rather than by locked doors, although in recent years it has become more common to define secure beds in terms of locked facilities. A second area of ambiguity arises because of overlap between secure 'treatment' and detention beds. Treatment beds provide for young people sentenced to the department. Detention beds are intended for young people awaiting a court hearing but are regularly used for those who have been committed. Ambiguity in terminology and practice may be useful as a device to ensure minimal usage, but it also carries the danger of gradual and almost imperceptible increases taking place. Clarification rather than ambiguity is part of Edward Murphy's management style, which has the merit of at least leading to agreement on the criteria for deciding which young people to lock up, even though disagreement remains as to what the maximum number should be.

These definitional difficulties arise when the development of secure provision is traced, and comparisons over the period since the early 1970s can only be approximate. In 1975 there were 105 secure treatment beds, of which seventy were within private programmes and relied more on staffing than physical security. In March 1980 there were seventy-nine secure treatment beds with another twelve about to become available. In January 1984 there were 103 secure treatment beds. These totals can be compared with two sets of recommendations. In 1977 the Harshbarger task force on secure care recommended that there be between 129 and 168 secure treatment beds (of which 29–38 should be administered by the Department of Mental Health, and 46–60 should provide less than full physical security). Four years later, in April 1981, Governor King's task force proposed that there should be a minimum of 326 secure treatment beds.

By 1984 little reference was made to Governor King's task force, and it was generally the Harshbarger recommendations which were quoted. As already detailed, only twelve secure beds were added between 1980 and 1984. A more substantial increase in provision was planned for 1984–7, taking the total number of secure beds to 184. Edward Murphy has commented that this total will not be far removed from the Harshbarger recommendation of secure provision for 11 per cent of the department's population. On the other hand, the Massachusetts Advocacy Center argued in 1980 that the ninety-one beds then available exceeded the outer limit of Harshbarger's lock-up requirements by twenty-one. Murphy reached his total of 184 by assuming that 26 per cent of commitments to the department are for crimes against the person and that half of this group require security.

Murphy has talked in terms of adding thirty or forty secure beds rather than twice that number, implied by his target for 1984. Murphy put the case as follows:

> To me this is a marginal change, one that is simply adjusting to changed circumstances and one in which, frankly, the department is trying to project to the citizenry here the fact that we are a credible agency in responding to juvenile crime. The degree to which we will be able to protect deinstitutionalization in the existing juvenile code in the future . . . to a large measure depends on our capacity to convince the public that we know what we're doing. If the addition of thirty or forty beds here manages to convince the public that we have those interests very much in mind, then to me I think that's a very beneficial result.

However, concerns about the planned expansion are raised in a draft departmental report, *The Classification Policies and Procedures*, Program Review (October 1983). Before reviewing the report's findings a brief description is required of the classification procedure. There are three major objectives, namely:

- To estimate the degree of risk and/or danger that the juvenile presents to the community and/or to him- or herself.

- To estimate the juvenile's actual and potential capability to modify his or her anti-social behaviour.
- To balance this assessment with the need to protect the community.

Classification of Offenders by Offense and Offense Behavior

Offense Category	Age Limit	Mandated Time Limits
MANDATORY REFERRALS: CATEGORY A		
Murder: First Degree	13–16 years	A minimum of twelve months to a maximum indeterminate stay. Length of time subject to periodic evaluation by treatment staff and legislation mandating release at age eighteen years, unless extension is granted by the court.
Murder: Second Degree		
Attempted Murder		
Voluntary Manslaughter		
MANDATORY REFERRALS: CATEGORY B		
Involuntary Manslaughter	14–16 years	A minimum of ten months to a maximum of fourteen months. Case conference can lead to early release or extension of maximum.
Armed Robbery		
Assault and Battery (armed) causing serious bodily injury		
Forcible Rape		
Arson of a Dwelling House		
Kidnapping		
Homicide by Motor Vehicle		

OPTIONAL REFERRALS

Any juvenile whose offense behavior presents a risk and danger to the community or who exhibits a persistent and escalating pattern of delinquency.	14–16 years	A range of months between a minimum of four months to a maximum of twelve months. Case conference can lead to early release or extension of maximum.

The above grid is applied to all commitments to DYS to determine whether the case will be referred to the Classification Panel for consideration for placement in a secure treatment program. To be eligible for classification the individual must:

(1) be at least 13 years of age and not yet 17 years;

(2) have been adjudicated as delinquent by the court;

(3) have committed any of the above offenses, or be considered a risk and danger to the community.

(Source: *Classification Policy Guidelines Concerning Entrance Into Secure Treatment Facilities*, 1982)

The procedure is as follows: all commitments by the court to DYS are reviewed by the regional director, who must determine whether the juvenile will be referred to the Classification Panel for possible admission to a secure setting. There are three categories of referrals: Mandatory A (homicide), Mandatory B (other serious violent offences), Optional (other offences).

The departmental study was based upon a quantitative analysis of all young people referred for secure placement during the year beginning May 1982. Of the 169 referrals 20 per cent had been involved in offences resulting in injuries requiring hospitalization; 13 per cent were violent offences without hospitalization; and 67 per cent of the offences were non-violent (or at least involved no injury). Specified serious offences result in mandatory referral; optional referrals, on the other hand, allow for considerable discretion by agency staff. The study found that 'it was clear in the case of some optional and revocation referrals that the criteria for the referral was not so much the offense history, but rather the youth's self-destructive behavior, failure in group or foster home placements, and frequent history of running and/or drug abuse, which provided the impetus for a referral to secure treatment'. The report recommends that the community-based system be examined 'to ensure that there are some alternatives available for a youth who may be disruptive for a time in a program, but who does not necessarily present a risk to the community'.

Noting the danger of inappropriate placement, the study warns: 'as the number of secure treatment beds increases, and the waiting lists diminish, it will be important to monitor for an increase in the number of optional referrals from the regions.' The study found that two thirds of referrals were optional or revocation cases and might not be considered a serious risk to the community, emphasizing 'the need for greater clarity on the criteria by which the majority of the youth are referred to secure treatment'.

As far as dispositional practice was concerned, the study found that 'the panel accepts some optional and revocation referrals who did not meet this criterion [risk to the community], but who did not appear stable enough to be placed in an open setting'. In one case, which illustrated the hard-to-place dilemma, a youth sentenced to DYS for stealing a bicycle, and whose subsequent offences were property crimes, had a history of running from programmes and drug abuse. He was not a risk to the community, but the case-worker was convinced he would run from any currently available programme. The study notes: 'One of the panel members expressed frustration with the lack of other alternatives for the youth in the community-based system.'

Most referrals were accepted by the panel. In fact the acceptance rate was higher in the case of optional and revocation cases than for A and B category cases. The study commented: 'Since the optional referrals are not necessarily of a serious offense history and are made at the region's discretion, it was of some surprise that the panel accepted 95 per cent of them.' It is clear that girls are treated differently from boys. In particular, in mandatory cases girls comprised only 15 per cent of all referrals. Most referrals were revocations, and the majority of girls were referred because their behaviour could not be controlled in an open setting. It was found that the number and type of proper resources for girls were much fewer than for boys. The study calculated a minimum cost (certain costs were not included) of $38,000 per annum per place and urged DYS 'to examine its regional community-based system to ensure all possible less expensive interventions are made with a youth prior to the last alternative of secure care'.

Murphy was much concerned about the enormous discretion employed by his department, especially regarding the use of secure beds. The procedures as described above, which have been in force since early 1981, structure intake procedures and decisions on duration of stay. Murphy had these procedures incorporated into the State Regulations Act which ensures that modifications require a public hearing. Murphy's second achievement with respect to secure provision has been to upgrade the quality of accommodation and programmes. When he made his first visit to the secure programmes he was 'scandalized by the quality of the plant'. Likewise, when Edward Loughran first visited the secure treatment programme at Roslingdale he said he was afraid for his life. Some secure programmes are located in buildings attached to rurally isolated state mental hospitals which are in the process of being phased out. It is not without irony that the decarceration of mental health made space available for DYS to provide both secure and other residential programmes. Roslingdale, which was opened in 1956 as a detention centre (i.e. for remand purposes), has for most of its existence been the subject of controversy. Miller later regretted that he never closed it. An occasion arose during the first Dukakis administration when it might have been closed, but this opportunity was not taken. Since April 1976 the facility has been subject to a consent decree ordered by a federal court, but there have been many difficulties in monitoring compliance to the decree's seventy-five provisions. In 1984 Roslingdale contained two secure treatment programmes (each with fifteen beds) and one detention programme (twenty-one beds). The immediate surroundings, given the facility's location between a graveyard and Boston's main mental hospital, are desperately bleak. Although based in the city the facility is isolated with one approach road closed to discourage dumping of garbage. One staff member has said that the setting is at its best when the garbage is covered by snow.

Edward Murphy regards the locked facilities in Massachusetts as providing the 'most humane security in the country'. The programmes are characterized by high staff ratios (about two staff to each resident), a relaxed level of interaction between staff and residents (especially apparent in the privately run programmes) and the relative absence of high-technology security paraphernalia. Considerable reliance is put on various points systems as a control device, thereby linking behaviour with privileges and comforts. Absconding from security facilities has been kept to an absolute minimum by means of well-resourced and professionally administered programmes.

Edward Murphy is adamant that the increase does not amount to slippage. Most supporters of the decarceration process in Massachusetts appear to share this view. Certainly there is no support for a return to large institutions. However, some concerns still exist about the scale of the planned increase in secure treatment provision. Jerry Miller, in his

Boston Globe article, raised questions about the development of secure programmes at a former girls' boarding school with the potential for two or three hundred beds. DYS officials insist that it will be limited to three programmes of fifteen beds each. Lloyd Ohlin, director of the Harvard research study on DYS, echoes these concerns, commenting that Murphy's 'clustering economy' carries the risk of large institutions.

Remand

Unlike most state juvenile corrections agencies, DYS has responsibility for the detention of young people remanded for court hearings.* Edward Murphy identifies detention practice and the difficulties of controlling the process as one of his most complex problems. Edward Loughran has underscored the issue by stating that 'detention drives the system'.

The court sets the level of bail but, while the amount has some influence, it does not determine placement, which is the responsibility of DYS. Jerry Miller closed the state's training schools but the detention centres remained. However, there was a one-third reduction in detention centre beds in the ten-year period up to 1984, when there were 108 beds (although the number of detention centres increased from four to seven). In 1980 the Massachusetts Advocacy Center identified secure detention as a major threat to the decarceration process. The Center found that eight out of every ten young people in detention centres were not on remand status but had been sentenced to the department. Most were runaways from programmes or were awaiting placement to a secure treatment unit. The Center's assessment was that in at least half of the cases detention was an

* In most states detention is the responsibility of county or city government.

inappropriate decision. The Center astutely observed that there is a financial incentive for DYS regional offices to use secure accommodation, including detention centres. Regions receive a purchase-of-service budget for community-based programmes, but secure provision is met by central office. 'The central office, therefore, has an incentive to keep fixed-cost programmes full' (Massachusetts Advocacy Center, 1980, p. 128).

More recent data on detention practice in Massachusetts were presented in a report by the Department of Youth Services. Based on nearly 600 cases over the first six months of 1983, the study found that 64 per cent of boys and 80 per cent of girls held in detention were released after trial. The report urged the development of state standards to govern closely the use of detention. The study did not deal with sentenced young people held in detention, an issue high-lighted by the Massachusetts Advocacy Center and by a review of national practice (Krisberg and Schwartz, 1983, p. 351).

The planned expansion in secure detention beds, from 108 to 130, is directly counter to the conclusion of the Massachu-setts Advocacy Center that the number of detention beds should be reduced substantially. It is recognized by senior DYS officials that additional beds will increase the temptation for courts to increase levels of bail. The department is planning to establish a pre-trial unit so as to improve data on the early stages of the process and to reduce the number of young people locked up in detention facilities. It is also held that there is greater sophistication among regional directors in dealing with the detention process. These developments should not mask the scope and complexity of the problems posed by the detention process. Success or failure in this area may be the crucial factor in determining whether decarcera-tion is advanced or retarded.

Transfer to the adult court

An indication of how judges and prosecutors regard the juvenile justice process is the extent to which juveniles on serious charges are 'bound over' or transferred to an adult court. Transfer arrangements vary among states, but the legislative trend across the United States has been to make transfers more likely. Some states have gone even further. In New York, for example, where the juvenile court has jurisdiction up to the age of sixteen, the Juvenile Offender Act of 1978 gave adult courts original jurisdiction over 13–15 year olds accused of any one of a lengthy list of serious offences.

Under Massachusetts law a young person aged between fourteen and sixteen may be transferred to an adult court if he or she has previously been committed to DYS and is charged with an imprisonable offence or is charged with an offence involving the infliction or threat of serious harm. If probable cause is found, the court will then consider, but is not limited to, evidence of the following factors:

- Seriousness of the alleged offence.
- The child's family, school and social history, including court and juvenile delinquent records, if any.
- Adequate protection of the public.
- The nature of any past treatment efforts for the child.
- The likelihood of rehabilitation of the child.

In 1976 a strict interpretation of the statute was decided by the Massachusetts Supreme Judicial Court, holding that:

We do not believe that a decision to transfer is proper when supported by findings which deal only with the seriousness of the charge and the inadequacy of existing juvenile facilities in terms of safeguarding the public. Despite the importance of these two factors and the weight that they may have in support of a conclusion that there should be a transfer to adult court, there must also be a finding that the juvenile cannot be rehabilitated within the present juvenile

93

structure or that, in the absence of long-term supervision and security, he poses a serious threat to the public, with subsidiary findings indicating the basis for this conclusion.*

It would appear that this decision by the Supreme Judicial Court in 1976, which was reinforced by subsequent decisions, contributed to a decline in transfers to adult courts, as shown in Table 2 below.

Table 2   Juvenile bindovers 1973–83

Year	Total
1973	129
1974	76
1975	126
1976	75
1977	36
1978	42
1979	47
1980	43
1981	36
1982	28
1983	27

The decline in bindovers has led to some suggestions – for example, by Governor King's Task Force in 1981 – that the statutory requirements should be made less restrictive. A more likely legislative change will be to give original jurisdiction to an adult court in the case of first-degree homicide (and perhaps other types of homicide, for example when caused by drunken driving). Representative Paul White's bill includes a provision for the Superior Court to have original jurisdiction for murder, manslaughter and motor vehicular homicide.

* A Juvenile v. Commonwealth, 370 Mass. 272, 280–283, 347 N.E. 2nd 677 (1976).

With respect to bindover practice Massachusetts shows every sign of having been more successful than most states in keeping juveniles out of the adult prison system. Since the early 1970s there have never been more than five persons under seventeen years of age in the adult correctional system.*

Strengthening programmes in the community

There is a considerable diversity of community-based programmes, ranging from highly structured residential settings to outreach and tracking programmes. The 'shelter' detention programme, situated in the grounds of the state mental hospital at Danvers, is run by the Northeastern Family Institute. Twenty-six full-time staff work with eighteen young people. There is no physical security, but every effort is made to discourage absconding. Very much less structured is the programme at Hastings House, a group home run by Massachusetts Halfway Houses Inc. The director is Michael Radan, who was held in one of the training schools at the time Jerry Miller was appointed commissioner. As Radan put it: 'I am thirty years old and have been seventeen years in the business.' Situated in a racially mixed neighbourhood in Cambridge, Hastings House has aroused few concerns within the community. 'We get less complaints from neighbours than the Massachusetts Institute of Technology fraternity house across the street,' commented Radan.

Situated in the Roxbury Boys' Club in the centre of the largely black district of Boston is an outreach and tracking programme administered by another private agency, Boston Basics Inc. The focus of the programme is educational and involves fifteen young people in a special school situation, preceded by breakfast. Some of the young people have shown a pattern of violence in the regular school system. Despite its

* Letter to the author from Professor Lloyd Ohlin, April 1984.

95

location, there is a multi-racial intake, with young people being collected by staff from their homes in various locations each morning. A certain level of support from the home is regarded as essential, and there are areas of the city, such as the desolate and mostly black public-housing area at Columbia Point, which the programme has failed to reach.

In the mid-1970s researchers at Harvard Law School, engaged in a major study of the decarceration process in Massachusetts, developed a new way of thinking about community-based programmes. It was suggested that, as well as focusing on the individual programme, it was useful to regard all existing programmes as a network with two main components:

High level of flexibility

The model assumes that young people's needs are not static or assessable in a highly prescriptive manner. A dynamic approach that recognizes the need for the provision of programmes and services on both sequential and simultaneous bases is often appropriate. The department, in its brokerage function, is involved in the complex task of co-ordination and monitoring. The model also assumes the active involvement by the individual young person in the selection of services and programmes.

An alternative to incarceration

At a broader level the model provides a useful perspective for approaching the task of developing alternatives to incarceration. Instead of regarding a single programme as an alternative to incarceration it may be more useful to think in terms of a network of programmes serving this purpose. Coates and his colleagues at the Harvard Center for Criminal Justice made a distinction between programme sets, programme strategies and individual programmes: a programme set is the total of all programmes designed to fulfil a given function; a programme strategy is the specific plan which defines goals at an operational level together with the means for achieving these goals; individual programmes are the means for implementing these strategies. The Harvard team was especially interested in the research implications of this perspective. They comment: 'Because of the rapid turnover of specific programmes in a changing correctional system, the different strategies become the principal focus for evaluation with the individual programmes (strategy components) becoming secondary' (Coates and Miller, 1975). If the major policy goal is to develop and sustain alternatives to incarceration, the operational task for the department is to put together the appropriate network of programmes. Failure to do this undermines the potency of any one programme to act as an alternative to secure custody, and this underlines the imperative that it is to community-based provision that DYS must now give its primary attention. Edward Murphy has acknowledged the implications of these considerations for the department: 'An effective community based system requires decentralized decision-making. Administrators must have sufficient confidence in their subordinates to delegate some of the organization's most important decisions to a level far removed from the central office' (Murphy, 1984, p. 6). The Harvard study has drawn attention to the distance which the department still has to go to integrate its work into the wider community:

Staff in most programs tend to try to do all the work themselves. They seem hesitant to involve the people of the community in either efforts to make youth want certain things or in efforts to make certain things happen. It is as if they do not trust anybody but themselves to take care of the youth. The result, of course, is that there is a failure to line the youth into any controls in the larger community that can outlast the youth's stay in the program. (Miller and Ohlin, 1983, p. 235)

Lloyd Ohlin has summed up the implications for policy and practice:

We only get effective treatment when we have some continuity of service with the family, with the school, with the neighbourhood system that builds in controls and supports. Those are the protections that those elderly people, and other potential victims, have to rely on, and they can do something about it, by trying to promote that kind of community assault on the problem.

Control over the private sector

Sixty per cent of the department's budget is for services contracted from private non-profit agencies. The original decision to encourage the private sector to provide alternative programmes was an important ingredient of the decarceration strategy, providing DYS with flexibility over a wide range of options. A perennial problem for DYS is to ensure quality control and develop an effective monitoring capacity. There are some eighty private non-profit agencies under contract to DYS, with contracts of between $120,000 and $800,000. In the mid-1970s fears were expressed that some private agencies had so grown as to impede the ability of DYS to insist that standards be met. By 1984, however, private agencies had come a long way in their sophistication in dealing with young people, and DYS had made some progress in controlling the private sector, both fiscally and in terms of programme quality.

The Federal Government

In the early 1970s federal grants played a crucial role in facilitating the switch of the DYS budget from institutions to the purchase of services. The events in Massachusetts gained support from some senior officials and legislators in Washington.

98

For example, in 1973 the National Advisory Commission on Criminal Justice Standards and Goals reported: 'The Commission believes that states should follow the example of Massachusetts, which has closed down statewide institutions for juveniles.' The following year decarceration was one of the priorities of the Juvenile Justice and Delinquency Prevention Act (see Rutherford, 1977). However, by the end of the decade the mood in Washington had shifted. For three successive years the Reagan administration attempted to cut off funds to the Office of Juvenile Justice and Delinquency Prevention which was established to implement the 1974 legislation. Congress has continued to fund the office, but the new administrator, Alfred Regnery, was unsympathetic to the 1974 legislative mandate. Regnery claims that during the 1970s the Office succeeded in removing juveniles from adult jails and 'status offenders' from incarcerative juvenile institutions,* and that now it has become appropriate to focus on the apprehension, prosecution and punishment of serious juvenile offenders. There has also been a shift in the Office's research priorities. It was decided in 1983 not to publish one of the federally funded final reports from the Harvard Law School on Massachusetts. Instead the Office has turned its attention to biologically oriented research into crime causation.

Emerging Issues in Massachusetts

Decarceration in Massuchusetts has survived and shows no sign of being reversed. In particular, Miller's legacy to the state emerged relatively unscathed from the four years of the

* But see Krisberg and Schwartz, who report: 'While the policy thrust to remove status offenders and non-offenders from secure institutions has proven to be a major success, the overall results with respect to deinstitutionalisation have been far less than what reformers had hoped for' (Krisberg and Schwartz, 1983, p. 357).

conservative King administration. Philip Johnston, senior advisor to Governor Dukakis, put it this way:

My conclusion at the end of the four years of King was that it was a tribute to Jerry Miller and everything that's been built up in this state over the last twelve years. Even as right wing a governor as Ed King was unable to destroy what had happened here, and my theory is that if Ed King can't do it nobody can. I guess that there just simply is no political constituency in this state for putting kids back into those large institutions; there's no one in the state, who's serious, who would favour a return to that system.

1. DYS and probation

A curious feature of juvenile justice trends in Massachusetts has been that sentences to DYS have risen since the late 1970s (although they fell in 1983) despite a decline in juvenile arrests. Juvenile arrests fell by 27 per cent between 1978 and 1982, largely reflecting demographic changes. Between 1970 and 1980 the number of 10–16 year olds in Massachusetts declined by 12 per cent and will drop a further 30 per cent between 1980 and 1990. As displayed in Table 3, the percentage decline in the number of juveniles appearing in court was twice the percentage fall in the juvenile population.

It can be seen from the table that the rate of first-time commitments to DYS per 1,000 juvenile arraignments rose from 24 to 44 in the years 1978–83. In part this increased use of DYS by the courts may reflect greater confidence in the level of services provided by DYS than, for example, by the Department of Welfare. Instead of being dealt with under a CHINS (Children in Need of Services) petition some young people may have been prosecuted.* A related consideration is the relative absence of services available to probation departments. As noted by the Governor's Anti-

* In 1974 responsibility for CHINS cases was transferred from DYS to the Department of Welfare.

Table 3 Numbers and rates of juveniles arraigned and first-time commitments to DYS 1978–82

Year	Number of juveniles aged 10–16	Number of juveniles arraigned	Arraignment rate per 1,000 juveniles	Number of first-time commitments to DYS	Committal rate per 1,000 arraignments
1978	718,599	28,419	39	686	24
1979	699,531	27,244	38	743	27
1980	671,675	25,943	39	854	33
1981	653,691	22,121	33	855	39
1982	627,487	20,799	33	863	41
1983	605,690	18,122	30	799	44
Percentage increase/ decrease 1978–83	−15·71	−36·23	−	+16·47	−

(Source: Juvenile Justice Committee of the Governor's Anti-Crime Council, 1983. Updated for 1983 by Commissioner Murphy)

Crime Council there is widespread agreement 'that a portion of the DYS commitment is caused by the way in which fiscal resources and commitments are structured in our juvenile justice system'. Arising from these concerns, initial steps are being taken to explore mechanisms which would shift fiscal resources in favour of probation services. Probation subsidy mechanisms in other states have been examined and, through the instigation of DYS, half a million dollars was made available in 1984 as a means to encouraging use of probation by the courts.* In effect this scheme provides the courts with their own purchase-or-services budget and may represent a first step in enhancing the effectiveness of probation in dealing with more serious offences.

* This sum is one third of what DYS requested and is not taken from the DYS budget.

2. Models for practice

The controversy arising from the events in Massachusetts has not been couched in terms of the traditional language of treatment and punishment approaches. The impetus for decarceration derived from pragmatic efforts to provide less-damaging environments for dealing with young people rather than from any particular theoretical position. The administrative discretion available to Jerry Miller to empty the training schools and for his successors to further the decarceration process derived from a treatment/welfare approach to juvenile justice, and this discretion was certainly counter to the just-deserts perspective which came to the fore during the 1970s. Both treatment and just deserts are regularly referred to in support of a particular measure. For example, the American Bar Association standards are invoked to support recommendations of the Massachusetts Advocacy Center regarding very tight detention usage but are not referred to by opponents of the direct sentencing issue. Programme staff often use treatment and even mental health terminology with reference to services and goals, whereas Edward Murphy is anxious to structure staff discretion to provide protections for young people.

As noted earlier, legislative efforts to give the courts direct sentencing powers have failed despite the persistent efforts of certain politicians and judges. A strong opposing voice is that of the Middlesex County District-Attorney, Scott Harshbarger:

> When the judges and probation officers get their act together and have uniform standards, and have specialized juvenile justice sessions, where they are relying on effective and consistent and comprehensive information, when we can be sure that the same judge in the same case, sitting in different parts of the state will determine roughly the same type of sentencing pattern, then we can seriously look at the question of should judges have the right to

determine what type of placement a juvenile should be in. But until then, very frankly, I think the pioneering concept here is that the placement of juveniles for purposes of correction, care and treatment is a speciality. There has to be some uniformity throughout the state and the single youth authority, the Department of Youth Services, I think, provides the most effective way to balance the limited number of facilities that are available with the need throughout the state. For example, in certain communities in the state a juvenile judge would like you to go to a secure facility for breaking and entering on your first or second offence, to teach you a lesson. That might be appropriate, but when we have limited facilities and we have in another part of the state a juvenile committing three armed robberies and is demonstrably dangerous to the public, then in a choice of who should have that facility I would like to have somebody look at the overall picture and determine which of these kids is the most dangerous to the public, and that can't happen through individual sentencing by judges.

Against this context it is somewhat surprising that in 1984 Edward Murphy proposed a complete revision of the state juvenile code. Almost eighty years after enactment of the existing code, Murphy believes that the underlying philosophical assumptions should be re-examined. These assumptions include the *parens patria* tradition of the juvenile court which was challenged but not outlawed by the US Supreme Court in cases such as *Gault* (1966). At Murphy's instigation the Juvenile Justice Committee of the Governor's Anti-Crime Council has recommended that a two-year code reform project be embarked upon. There are some observers who have concerns that this effort might lead to a legislative free-for-all. Others regard the exercise as irrelevant to more immediate issues such as increasing resources for community-based programmes. In particular there is the question of whether enough is being done to explore new ways of approaching young people involved in crime – ways that harness resources within the family, school and neighbourhood. What more might be done to foster the pace of learning and innovation which was given impetus by the events of the early 1970s?

For Jerry Miller the department's emphasis should be on providing growth-producing opportunities for young people in trouble. He is convinced that this cannot be done within an incarcerative institution because that is not what one would choose for one's own child.

I do believe, to a degree, in the perfectability of man, and I think that the best model I could use is what I would insist upon doing for my own were they in trouble, and I think that if we use that as the measure we would be in quite good shape, because we get very innovative, very creative when our own get in trouble, particularly if we're given the amount of money that the state spends to incarcerate youngsters that are in trouble. And I think one then moves into an entirely different realm. This idea that delinquents are somehow or other qualitatively different than the rest of us, or that our own have no propensity or possibility or potential for involving themselves in similar or worse behaviour, is nonsense. And the criminal justice system has had a long history and tradition of separating us one from another, of scapegoating, of stereotyping, of providing the definitions that allow us to exclude our fellow human beings from the human family, and I think to the degree that we design correctional systems they should be healing for the society as well, and hopefully that's what we accomplished in Massachusetts, at least to some small degree.

Conclusions

Concerns remain with the expansion of secure treatment and detention beds and the neglect of community-based provisions. Nevertheless, the strength of the Massachusetts decarceration process is especially apparent in the context of what happened elsewhere in the United States during the decade up to 1985. Brief mention has been made of the shift in emphasis within the federal government with reference to juvenile justice priorities: a shift from decarceration to strengthened prosecution and sentencing of more serious offenders. This change of climate is reflected in terms of institutional closures. Lloyd Ohlin commented that the Massachusetts training schools were closed at 'the tail end of '60s and early '70s' and probably occurred just in time. Had the events taken place in the early 1960s their replication beyond Massachusetts would have been more likely.*

In terms of admissions to training schools during the period 1974–9, twenty-five states showed increases and twenty-five showed decreases. The declines were largely accounted for by fewer 'status' offenders being institutionalized. Similarly the overall decline in admissions to detention was largely accounted for by status offenders. One review of these national data implicitly endorses the logic of the Massachusetts deep-end strategy and argues that custodial capacity must be reduced: 'Diversion and alternative programmes have mushroomed while detention rates declined only slightly and training school admission rates not at all' (Krisberg and Schwartz, 1983).† Massachusetts in 1982 had the lowest incarceration rate of juveniles in the nation (taking account of detention centres and youth institutions). For the US as a whole the rate was 134 per 100,000 juveniles compared with a rate for Massachusetts of 13 per 100,000.‡ Jerry Miller sought a process of juvenile justice in Massachusetts which would resist efforts at reversal by Heinrich Himmler. Miller's colourful comment should not distract from

* Although significant decarceration steps have been taken in Utah and Iowa.

† It was also found that 77 per cent of the variation between states in the use of detention could be explained in terms of the number of detention beds. The comparable explanatory percentage for training schools was 27 per cent (but this represented 82 per cent of all the variation that was explained by the selected independent variables).

‡ *Rethinking Juvenile Justice: National Statistical Trends*, Minneapolis, Hubert H. Humphrey Institute of Public Affairs, 1984.

the recognition that the response to young people and crime in Massachusetts represents an oasis in the United States. The process of decarceration in Massachusetts has largely survived the conservative law-and-order mood which has swept much of the country since the mid-1970s.

When Jerry Miller left Massachusetts in January 1973 he had been commissioner of youth services for less than forty months. He went on to hold senior appointments at a state level in Illinois and Pennsylvania, but powerful groups with investments in the status quo were able to organize effective opposition. On taking up his appointment as director of the Illinois Department of Children and Family Services he was told that youth correction would be transferred from the prison system to his agency. This never happened, and a decline in political support culminated in his transfer to a position in the governor's office. In January 1975 he joined the staff of Governor Milton Shapp of Pennsylvania (as director of community-based programmes) and in May of that year became Commissioner of the Office of Children and Youth within the Department of Public Welfare. He developed the brokerage role for both these state agencies. In Illinois a federally funded programme, Unified Delinquency Intervention Services (UDIS), provided an array of programmes for the young people of Chicago as an alternative to placement in state training schools. In Pennsylvania federal funds supported the Camp Hill Project, which developed a network of programmes to replace the incarceration of some 400 juveniles in an adult state prison (McGillis and Spangenberg, 1976). In 1977 he founded an agency which works with defence counsel in providing sentencers with alternatives to imprisonment. In exile, Miller, the ultimate reluctant bureaucrat, waits in vain for a call to return to the crusade. Meanwhile, in Massachusetts the training schools remain closed, and the state is able to address itself to the problems

106

of youth crime, unhindered by the irrelevant heritage of juvenile prisons.

The work which remains to be done in Massachusetts in no way diminishes the significance of the gains that have been made. Lloyd Ohlin has summed up the key lesson as being confirmation of Jerry Miller's faith in not over-reacting to teenage behaviour, reflecting 'an extraordinarily generous willingness to look at each offender as someone trapped by events, someone who is not an event but a person'. Ohlin concludes that incarceration is a deceptive policy which over the long term will inevitably fail, and that only in the community can the problem of youth crime be effectively tackled.

The first state training school in the United States was opened in Massachusetts in 1846. One hundred and twenty-six years later this and other training schools in Massachusetts were abandoned. Beyond Massachusetts the decarceration task is as urgent as it is formidable.*

* The total numbers held in juvenile institutions in the United States fell from 77,000 to 72,000 between 1974 and 1979, but by 1982 had increased to 80,000. 'There is no solid evidence that these policies of increased juvenile incapacitation are positively affecting public safety' (B. Krisberg et al., 'The watershed of juvenile justice reform', Hubert H. Humphrey Institute of Public Affairs, 1985).

Chapter Four

Holding On

Unless schools, parents and social workers are prepared to tolerate a certain amount of disturbance, in the confident expectation that most youngsters will grow out of their troublesome phase, and unless they are prepared to tackle some of the more difficult problems themselves, instead of exporting them to an over-burdened penal system, legal formulae for 'diversion' will be so much waste of paper. (Donald West, 1982, p. 146)

●

Management of young people and crime has to be rescued from criminal justice and other types of formal intervention and returned to where it belongs. The key question for policy-makers is how to foster and support the capacity of homes and schools to respond effectively and hold on to young people in trouble. The financial resources of homes and schools are only part of the requirement. The crucial ingredient is the level of personal support and commitment offered to young people.

Without question, some everyday practice leads policy with respect to the developmental approach to youth crime. Much can be learned from the skill and determination of those parents and teachers who hold on to their young people, and from practice within the criminal justice arena which seeks to strengthen the community's capacity to manage young people and crime. Policy on youth crime has been retarded by a failure to build on the lessons of successful practice.

108

Holding On at Home

The Black report on services for young people in Northern Ireland succinctly identified the importance of the family:

The family is the first and most basic institution in our society for developing a child's potential . . . It is within the family that the child experiences love, attention, care, supervision, discipline, conflict, neglect, stress or abuse depending on parental and family characteristics and circumstances . . . Society must seek to develop and provide the environment, resources and opportunities through which families can become more competent to deal with their own problems. (Black, 1979, pp. 6–7)

Among problems with which the family may have to grapple are the young person's involvement in criminal and other troubling escapades. A critical aspect of bringing up children is the provision of support and control, especially during periods of difficult behaviour.

Levels of control and support provided within the home depend upon many considerations, not least social circumstances and resources including the availability of an extended family. Social deprivation has been suggested by many studies as a factor within the home that is associated with crime. Donald West, for example, regards social deprivation as 'an agglomeration of interacting factors' and points to 'its aftermath, the antisocial syndrome' (West, 1982, pp. 117–19). But regardless of social and economic circumstances there are variations of styles of parental supervision, and these appear to be associated with the extent to which young people get involved in crime. Parental supervision, one study suggests, is a 'protective measure against delinquency [which] appeared to operate effectively among disadvantaged families resident in deprived inner-city areas' (Wilson, 1980, p. 204). Furthermore, social deprivation is not inherently associated with youth crime, as noted in a review of Swedish research: 'This steep rise in criminality [which has mainly involved young persons] has accompanied a rapid rise in national standards of material well-being.' It was suggested that this type of 'affluence criminality' is the consequence of a decline in informal social controls, resulting from 'the totally transformed role of teenagers in modern society. The most important element of this transformation is the transition from a producer to a consumer role. Young persons today are not subject to the preventive control formerly entailed by working together with adults' (Sarnecki, 1983, p. 2).

The importance of social circumstances to the capacity of the home to hold on to a young person in trouble is far from straightforward. To a considerable extent social and economic considerations determine whether options to criminal justice intervention are available to families. Some of these options, however, also lead to incarcerative institutions. Access to private secure psychiatric facilities makes middle-class young people especially vulnerable. As noted by two American sociologists: 'a social control perspective predicts, for adolescents, the separation of class origins from power and resources . . . The middle-class adolescent is more liable to "voluntary" incarceration than the lower-class adolescent' (Guttridge and Warren, 1984, p. 23).

The following account by Carole of a winter with Rick, her fifteen-year-old son, describes an unremarkable family crisis met with fortitude and perseverance.

A winter's tale

'September is always the beginning of a new year in our lives. School starts and Rick says everything is "alright". By the end of October I'm vaguely aware that Rick is doing less and less homework, but *I'm not really paying attention*. What he is

110

spending all the hours doing at home is secluding himself in his room on the phone. His social life clearly reigns supreme. Then in November his weekend behavior begins to get erratic. He goes to the skating rink but breaks every curfew – not by minutes but by hours. And for the first time in his life, he is becoming a pathological liar. He is absolutely *never* where he says he's going to be; he stays out all night, spending it at other kids' houses without even calling to let us know (and he not even yet sixteen); or sneaks into our house at 3.30 a.m. with two other boys who spend the night without letting their parents know. So every Friday night he would do something outrageous, which would keep us up all night long, result in our grounding him for the rest of the weekend, and require us to stay home the rest of the weekend to watch him, talking about his problems and ringing our friends. The atmosphere in our household had become exclusively high tension and anger. It was affecting Doug badly, he telling us we were always down on Rick. Doug began biting his nails vigorously. Doug also began lying to cover up Rick's sins of omission and commission.

'This awful state of affairs continued into January (including Christmas). Stan and I were sleeping miserably and spending our days obsessed with what to do about Rick, how to force, cajole or otherwise get him to take more responsibility for his own life, his obligations to his own future and to his family.

'By now I knew Rick was flunking (as in F's) his three key academic courses. And he was surely flunking the bigger course, *life*. We decided to investigate private schools, alerting Rick that if he didn't turn around at home and in school by the end of the semester we would have to send him to boarding-school, where discipline is enforced and where self-discipline is taught in ways more effective than we had apparently taught it. To that end we wrote, called and read about a dozen schools, and ultimately visited, with Rick, three, in early January. All three essentially said to us: "Look, if you can't be more specific about what his learning disabilities are, we cannot place Rick. Perhaps you should go have him tested and diagnosed again, and then get back to us with the results."

'So on 21 January, he spent eight hours in testing (and $495.00) at a place of excellent repute. They concluded that his language abilities are in the below-average range, that his math abilities indicate a fundamental learning disability, that his fear of being sent to boarding-school was so profound it would probably be counter-productive, that we should first try professional tutoring (which the Center would provide), and that the most we could expect of Rick was D's in regular classes.

'By now, his report card came with an F in English, F in Biology, D in Math, and even a D in Driver's Ed (success in which he clearly had an incentive). His English and Biology teachers, in conference with his counselor and me, were strongly urging that he be removed from their classes, as he hadn't even attempted the work in months! The counselor agreed. However, it also was revealed in this conference that Rick had been erroneously assigned in both these classes – that they were accelerated classes for bright students, and he was supposed to have been assigned to a lower English and Biology course last September. I wanted to commit homicide on the counselor, right there, but she being in power and me being only a parent, I thought better of it!

'I went home and explained the whole nasty mistake to Rick, told him we all wanted to reassign him to easier classes where he'd have a better chance at *experiencing success*, and he dug in his heels and said: "No. I am sick and tired of being in Learning Disabled classes, of the embarrassment and the label; I want to be like my friends. And I'd rather try to get a D in a hard class than a C or B in an easier one. No!"

'At this same time came one other little diversion. I came

home from work one day in late January, to be informed by Rick that he'd been picked up by the police that afternoon. His story was that he'd been fooling around with his friend, outside the local grocery store, in a mock karate fight and had *accidentally* kicked another boy, a total stranger, who'd come by. And his friend had punched another boy, also a stranger. Further, the night before he had pushed the "victim's" brother in a snow bank, for calling Rick a name. So Stan and I were to go to the police station with Rick on Saturday morning. Go we did, to an interrogation room, where the policeman revealed that the victim's parents were pressing charges of *assault* against Rick for kicking the boy. The boy, it was admitted, was not hurt, did not fall down, but his parents wanted to teach Rick a lesson. My heart was in my throat because I felt certain that all the "I don't know" responses Rick was giving to the policeman's questions were not true. So did the police, who told Rick he'd better not commit perjury when the case came before juvenile court. Rick is visibly scared to death, I'm shaking, Stan is tearing at his beard, and we all go home and grill Rick for the rest of the weekend. Stan and I decide that if this really does go to court, we'll let the chips fall where they may, to teach Rick a lesson about controlling his anger and exercising good judgement.

'Nothing happens for three months on the legal front, but by late January Rick tells us he believes his life has hit an all-time low, that he can't get any lower, and that he is prepared to turn it around. He still says he wishes we would give him more credit for never taking drugs or alcohol (which *all his friends* do) but other than that merit, he counts among his demerits an inability to keep his friends, flunking in school, being always in trouble at home, and now in trouble with the law. He also analyzes his behavior over the past months, and decides that as soon as he had gotten a little behind and befuddled in his classes, he felt so overwhelmed and hopeless about it he totally quit trying.

'So in early February I started having weekly meetings with his teachers, getting from them the course outlines, lesson plans, schedules of exactly what would be due and when. I bought material to use for the study of skeletal, muscular, circulatory, respiratory and digestive systems (all of which would be covered in the next quarter). I worked with Rick every night for two hours, reteaching him study skills, and relearning (for me) human and animal biology, interpreting *Julius Caesar*, teaching him how to take notes when he read a novel for a book report, or a research paper. And the tutor worked with him two afternoons a week. Hosanna! The homework, quizzes and tests started coming back with A's, A-, B+ and notes of congratulations to him from his teachers. The better he did the better he thought he could do. His 3rd Quarter Report Card came home last week: from F to B in English, from F to B+ in Biology, from D to C+ in Math, from D to B in Physical Education.

'The only cloud in this improving picture is that a real live summons appeared from juvenile court the last week in March, requiring Rick's appearance in mid-April. We all begin to get scared anew, and Stan and I decide we'd better not just let the chips fall where they may. Stan takes Rick to see a lawyer, who had previously been a policeman and a prosecuting attorney for juvenile court. He is now a defense attorney who knows more than we could ever have imagined about the juvenile justice system. You've already heard what can go wrong with the education system (not to mention the "parenting system"). Now read what can go wrong with the juvenile justice system. The parents, we learn, have charged Rick twice: one for a kick, and one for pushing the brother in the snow bank. The lawyer says the judge can sentence Rick to jail, and some judges have for similar offenses. Or, worse yet, he can put Rick on probation (including a 10.00 p.m. curfew) for a year or two. If Rick were to miss that curfew by five minutes once, a bitter cynical probation officer could have him sent to a detention home, where he would live with juvenile rapists and murderers. Or he might get a suspended sentence. Any of those three outcomes result in Rick having a record until he's eighteen, clearly impeding his employability. The lawyer is brutally honest with Rick and Stan, and holds the system in disrepute.

'Stan and Rick decide to retain this lawyer, who says his first move will be to try to persuade the family to drop the charges. They drive home and relate all this to me, with Rick crying all the way home in the car. For the past three weeks, then, all any of us have been able to think about is the possible outcome of this trial. And the more we think about it, the more outrageous it seems that a teenager could get charged with assault for pushing another teenager in the snow. Somehow, that charge began to deprive dignity from the kicking charge.

'To end this story, the trial was Monday. The lawyer explained to the family the situation Rick was in when this happened back in January (the anger, the failure, the prospect of being sent away from home to boarding-school), and the extent to which Rick had turned himself around since then. They were initially resistant to dropping the charges (they wanted to set an example to their sons and had taken other teenagers to court before) but even the policeman urged them to do so. They finally agreed, so the judge did also. Rick apologized to the two boys and we all breathed a huge sigh of relief.

'It's spring. The new quarter has started and we're all proceeding with renewed hope and optimism. Rick hasn't broken a curfew since January, has a cute girlfriend whose mother adores him. He's away at the beach with them this weekend.'

Rick's story highlights the enormous potential within the home to hold on to the young person in trouble, where there is the will and ability to harness resources and a strong and consistent commitment to the young person. The account contrasts to situations where parents decide, for reasons which include the sheer scale of difficulties, tensions or lack of resources, that they cannot or will not hold on.* In these circumstances, and in others where intervention becomes inevitable, the difficulty for policy-makers is how to assist the home in harnessing resources and to avoid actions which weaken the capacity of the home to hold on.

The contrasting policy perspectives of Denmark and Sweden are instructive. In Denmark, where raising children is regarded as primarily the job of the family, guidance is available which supplements but does not replace the family's responsibilities. In Sweden, where the developmental role of the family has become weaker, the agencies of government have sought to give 'parents and children freedom to create their own lives within the larger "family" of Swedish society' (Tempkin, 1973). Sweden pioneered boarding out or fostering of young people as an alternative to incarcerative institutions. Nancy Hazel and others in England have demonstrated that when used appropriately the foster home may have much to offer: 'Many adolescents are rejected by their parents, and delinquent or unacceptable behaviour both reflects and confirms this rejection. During placement, relationships with the family of origin tend to become more amicable, probably because the pressure of guilt is eased on both sides' (Hazel, 1978, p. 95). Hazel's social network of professionals and foster-parents which provides support and encouragement may be the type of arrangement that is required to keep young people in their own homes. If foster-parents routinely require support, can anything less be justified to see parents through a troubled phase?

* The importance of child–parent relationships is emphasized by Riley and Shaw (1985) in their research report which appeared as this book was going to press.

Holding On in Schools

The most important developmental institution outside the home is the school. Given the amount of time young people spend at school during their formative years, it is hardly surprising that research findings show schools having an impact upon pupils' behaviour beyond academic achievement. Since the late 1960s a series of studies have found that differences in truancy and offending patterns across schools cannot be entirely accounted for by variations in pupil intake. Michael Power's studies of London schools made this point with some force (Power et al., 1967, 1972), but his proposal to examine how the schools accounted for the differences was blocked by the Inner London Education Authority and the National Union of Teachers. Further research in London by Michael Rutter and in South Wales by David Reynolds confirmed Power's findings, and they were able to investigate how schools differed. Rutter's study of twelve comprehensive schools serving inner London produced these main findings:

- There were marked differences in attainments and behaviour.
- The differences in intake did not wholly account for these differences.
- The variations remained stable over a 4–5 year period.
- The different forms of success were closely connected.
- The outcome differences were not due to physical factors or to differences in administration or organization.
- The differences *were* systematically related to characteristics of the school as a social organization; these were factors which could be modified by staff.
- The outcomes were also influenced by factors outside the control of teachers, in particular the academic balance in the intakes to the schools; the effect of this balance was most marked with respect to delinquency.

117

- It seems that it is the school's particular ethos (set of values, attitudes, behaviours which characterize the school) that has greatest impact on pupils.
- A causal process appears to be at work whereby to an appreciable extent children's behaviour and attitudes are shaped and influenced by their experiences at school and, in particular, by the qualities of the school as a social institution (Rutter et al., 1979, p. 179).

Rutter explored the notion of ethos in detail, noting differences in disciplinary styles within the classroom and expectations of teachers regarding pupils. He comments: 'Schools which expected children to care for their own resources had better behaviour, better attendance and less delinquency . . . The message of confidence that the pupils can be trusted to act with maturity and responsibility is likely to encourage pupils to fulfil those expectations' (Rutter et al., 1979, p. 188). Also of importance were the example set by teaching staff, rewards and punishment, and the degree to which staff acted together to develop a school-wide set of values.

Rutter suggests that, contrary to expectations, he found that the pupil mix most strongly predisposed to delinquency was not a mix of boys with the highest individual predisposition to delinquency, but one where there was a heavy preponderance of the least able. He suggests that the explanation may in part lie in the effects of scholastic failure on feelings of personal worth leading to anti-school peer groups. Nor was any particular style of leadership by headteachers important; indeed, the heads of the more successful schools took widely different approaches. Rutter suggests that these headteachers had essential elements in common which remain to be identified. Rutter concludes that schools can do much to promote good behaviour and attainments and that, even in a disadvantaged area, schools can be a force for the good (Rutter et al., 1979, p. 205).

The results of the London study are usefully complemented by research in South Wales. The eight schools studied by David Reynolds served a relatively homogeneous former mining valley and, again, pupil intake did not fully account for the variation between the schools. Factors associated with the more 'effective' regimes included a high proportion of pupils in authority positions; low levels of institutional control; low rates of physical punishment; small overall size; more favourable teacher/pupil ratios; and more tolerant attitudes to enforcing rules on 'dress, manners and morals'. Reynolds concluded that schools differ in the strategies used to mobilize pupils towards acceptance of school purposes. In broad terms, these strategies can be described as incorporation and coercion. Incorporation involves pupils in the organizing of the school and eliciting parental support. Pupils are encouraged to take an active part in the classroom and in extra-curricular activities, discouraging anti-school attitudes. Pupils getting into trouble evoke therapeutic rather than coercive responses within the school. By contrast, in the coercive schools there was little tolerance of acting-out by pupils. In these schools (three of the eight) teachers anticipated that pupils would take advantage of leniency. Reynolds suggests that contrasting perceptions by teachers of pupils provide the most likely explanation as to choice of strategy. These perceptions, in turn, become self-fulfilling prophecies. Reynolds suggests that the key to successful changes in school practice lies in the interpersonal relations and mutual perceptions of teachers and pupils. Of paramount importance is the school's ethos rather than its organizational structure (Reynolds and Sullivan, 1981).

These studies have implications for explorations of schools' potential to cope with young people in trouble. The incorporative school will do what it can to hold on to disruptive, delinquent or truanting pupils because it regards them in positive terms. It believes that the school should not fail its pupils, and that it has something of value to offer. Furthermore, it enjoys the confidence of police and courts. Schools not only differ in the behaviour of their pupils but in the determination and the ability of the school to prevent or reduce contact between their pupils and criminal justice.

It is often the disruptive rather than the truanting child who most upsets teachers. With such children a groundswell of opinion may develop among the staff to get them out of the school. Ways of achieving this include suspension or expulsion and propelling the young person in the direction of the police and the courts. The groundswell for getting rid of the child is especially likely when teachers see their job as strictly educational rather than in pastoral terms, or where the pupil is used by teachers as a means of taking on the headteacher.

Powers to suspend and expel pupils derive not from statute but from the school's articles of government. The rate of suspension varies greatly from one school to another, and one source of variance may be that some heads and their staff have developed ways in which they are able to deal with pupils within the school setting. The governor of a London school has written that her 'strong impression is that the whole issue of pupils "in trouble" is the least satisfactory part of the authority's services' (Monck, 1983, p. 7). The range and quality of provision for troublesome pupils are considerable. In some areas extensive arrangements have been created, ranging from special units, where the child may or may not finish his or her schooling, to home tutors. Very often the provision exists only on paper. Such arrangements are expensive and rarely sufficient to meet demand. Furthermore, they are not able to offer pupils involved a full curriculum. Thus there are both economic and educational pressures on authorities to restrict such special provisions. The Inner London

Education Authority, for example, has encouraged headteachers to limit suspensions by tightening up on the formal procedures. It also keeps a close watch on how many pupils each school suspends. Under this pressure, some headteachers who are unwilling or unable to cope with the disruptive child within the school setting may more readily seek a solution through the courts. A custodial sentence achieves a 'suspension' without upsetting the Authority, and the headteacher achieves a low suspension rate. Another way headteachers can get rid of pupils without using formal suspension, and often for much longer periods, is to arrange for them to be directly admitted to the variety of special units. There are usually strict screening procedures involving the school's psychological service, but the influence of the headteacher remains paramount. It is not unusual for a large inner London secondary school to have twenty or thirty or more pupils on its 'special register'. These pupils count on the school roll and thus contribute towards the allocation of resources to the school (both human and physical) yet, in practice, attend other institutions, usually on a full-time basis. The allocation of resources on account of pupils who do not actually attend the school is clearly an encouragement for headteachers to build up their special registers. In London, for example, a special register of thirty-four pupils would entitle the school to two extra members of staff. Since the thirty-four pupils would be educated elsewhere, these two members of staff could be deployed entirely within the school for the benefit of the remaining pupils. This could be justified if the pupils attended these units on a short-term and preferably part-time basis, but this is not normally the case. All too often the special units are seen as a means of permanently excluding difficult pupils.

As already noted, the school may encourage prosecution and removal from home in order to conserve resources. The two key points of contact between the school and criminal justice are with the police, when prosecution is being considered, and with the courts, when a report is requested to assist the sentencing decision.

Contacts between school and police

Arrangements usually exist for consideration by the police of the views of the school on whether or not to prosecute. This may be a formal process, such as the juvenile liaison scheme, where input is sought from the school, or it may be informal. In the latter case the initiative may be taken by the school. In cases of assault, robbery and theft within the school, the police generally require the victim to take out the prosecution. Where the victim is a child, this decision is usually taken by the parents, who tend to rely on the advice of the headteacher, taking account of the extent to which the headteacher is willing to deal with the matter him- or herself. The practice of headteachers varies greatly, and headteachers are not usually provided with any guidance. Some headteachers are keen to encourage prosecution whenever possible; others are equally keen to discourage it.

Those who are quick to involve the police may do so out of a belief that crime is the province of the courts, or they may be influenced by practical considerations. Serious incidents in school can take up a great deal of time and effort on the part of senior staff. Investigation of the incident, written reports, interviews with parents, implementation of corrective action or punishment can take a heavy toll. By calling in the police, some heads are thereby able to avoid this unwelcome distraction.

It seems likely that the most creative efforts to hold on to pupils are made in the private sector. It is not unusual for the private school to assure the police that it is able to take effective steps to deal with the matter or, at most, that a formal caution by the police may be useful. The private school may make assurances that the child will be moved to another school elsewhere in the country, or will be gated (i.e. kept in the school), or that the victim has been recompensed and sees no need for prosecution. The private school may develop good informal relations with the police at senior level ensuring that incidents are smoothly dealt with as they arise.

An example of formal working arrangements between police and the school is where headmasters are invited to attend the weekly meeting of the juvenile liaison panel which is also attended by education welfare officers and other professionals. In at least one school, information will be lodged in the child's file and a form tutor will invite the pupil to talk about the trouble he or she is in, offering the school's help and support to the pupil and parents where possible. This school's headteacher has emphasized that the matter must not be broached where other children are present – that it must be brought up in a counselling capacity and with total confidentiality (Pask, 1982). This degree of sensitivity is not always present. For example, Lancashire police have decided, as a general rule, not to inform schools that a child has been cautioned, as senior police officers became concerned about cases of pupils who were identified as thieves in front of school assembly or by their names being written on a blackboard (Laugharne, 1983).

Schools and courts

The second main type of contact between schools and criminal justice is the report prepared by the school for the court. A review of forms used by forty education authorities found that in only one case was the school specifically asked what might be said in favour of the child. It has been suggested that the quality of pastoral care within a school can be measured by its school reports (Ball, 1982).

One headmaster has written with reference to school

reports: 'There is a strong temptation (to which teachers quite often yield, if evidence collected nationally is to be believed) to use the school report to the court as a forum for the expression of frustration, or even irritation and anger towards the child, especially in cases where the child is a nuisance at school. In some cases there is a temptation for us to claim that we had "foreseen this all along". In yet other cases we might even feel that our chance has come to get rid of a troublemaker. All such temptation must be resisted. No matter how irritating a child may be, how aggravating or aggressive his presentation, a juvenile before the court is in distress and, most commonly, has been failed to one degree or another by the adults responsible for his/her care' (Pask, 1982). Not only may the school seek prosecution but it may also seek to encourage the court to use its most severe powers and thereby rid itself of the young person. A deputy headteacher has noted:

Many teachers see custodial provision as the ultimate sanction and they often express disappointment when a supervision order or community service is recommended. There is clearly a lot of in-service work to be done here. The school could play a valuable role in the developing policy of diverting juveniles from the courts, if teacher attitudes were to change. (Maher, 1984, p. 10)

The school report often reveals much about the school's level of support for the young person involved. In some instances the language is graphic in the extreme: 'This boy exercises an Al Capone influence in the playground'; and, 'Jimmy is a cancer to the student body – if he didn't commit this offence, then someone else in his family did'; 'The school has failed in its persistent efforts to exercise proper control over Derek . . . We recommend that Derek is shown that his disregard for the ordinary rules of behaviour will not go unpunished and in spite of the fact that it seems unthinkable for someone of Derek's inadequacy to go to detention centre, this is what we feel forced to recommend'; and finally, 'This boy is big, black and smelly' (NACRO, 1984, pp. 10–11).

There is considerable ambiguity in the rules governing juvenile court proceedings as to whether or not reports prepared by schools be shown to parents and/or the child. In a survey of all justices' clerks, Caroline Ball found:

Changes [only 9 per cent of courts were said to have changed their practice over the past five years] towards showing [reports] appear to have been instigated almost equally by magistrates and justices' clerks, whilst moves towards greater restriction were reported as having been made mainly as a result of requests to courts by headteachers, who are generally perceived by clerks as being jealous of the confidentiality of their reports. (Ball, 1983, p. 201)

Several clerks commented to the effect that when headteachers discovered that courts were showing their reports they 'were not at all pleased and, following a meeting, the practice was changed'. However, in one instance the change was in the opposite direction, at the instigation of a headteacher. Ball reported that where the change had been towards greater restriction, the indication was that reports were fuller and more detailed, but that when the change was in the opposite direction the reverse was not observed. One court clerk noted: 'Staff room gossip had gone but frankness of reports was uninhibited.' Caroline Ball concluded: 'With the collusion of clerks and juvenile panel justices, this has resulted in the current situation where a number of juvenile courts could, on good grounds, be open to charges of administering "secret justice" ' (Ball, 1983, pp. 8–10).

The school's report to court is a strategic document which, as Henri Giller suggests, often imputes blame rather than placing the pupil in a favourable light (Giller, 1982, pp. 4–6). This tendency has been commented on by a headmaster:

125

Subject tutors' comments should not be reproduced in detail except where this may help to obtain a particular positive outcome. In many cases the subject reports may simply reiterate a child's failures or difficulties and therefore do him or her down. There should always be a positive side to the school report. This school is committed to the view that all youngsters should be given some success and invited to build on it. I have never known a young person for whom some success or something positive could not be identified. (Pask, 1982, p. 6)

Considerations concerning school reports to court raise questions about the scope and objectives of educational settings. The school is concerned not only with academic achievement but also with preparing young people for the society and world in which they are growing up. The school's pastoral role has gained significance with the relative shift of influence over young people away from the family. James Coleman, in exploring this transition, noted: 'This absorption of adolescent time by the school has contributed to the dominance of the student role among the many roles that a young person might have. This family role has been diminished as the family has declined in size and strength' (Coleman et al., 1974, p. 80; see also Rutter and Giller, 1983, pp. 329–30).

The school's pastoral role involves watching over the pupil's development and recognizing opportunities to provide support when the young person is in trouble. Pastoral responsibilities are often neglected because, as Peter Maher comments, many teachers take an insular view of their profession. Very little of teachers' initial training deals with pastoral care (Maher, 1984, p. 2). Schools vary in the priority placed on pastoral responsibilities. Coleman has argued that the large American high school has failed to meet the diverse nature of the challenge: 'There are limits on how comprehensive any educational organization can be without blandness eroding all sense of purpose and enterprise.' Coleman and his colleagues urged changes in the school's structure, so that it might address more than a narrow range of tasks (Coleman et al., 1974, p. 146). The pastoral role is commonly recognized in the private sector, where personal tutors keep a watchful eye over particular pupils and, when necessary, are in close contact with their parents. In the state school system there are often obstacles owing to resistance by teachers and the expectations of young people and their parents. Howard Parker, in his appreciative study of working-class youth in Merseyside, writes: 'The Boys treated school as simply a process they were involuntarily put through.' He noted that several of his group had passed the 11+ exam but were unable to handle the grammar school situation (Parker, 1974, pp. 197–200). Mutual stereotyping, self-fulfilling prophecies and cynically negative attitudes contribute to the sometimes herculean nature of the task of releasing the school's capacity as a developmental institution.

Home and school, and places of further education, may continue to provide the protection of the developmental institution up until the early twenties and sometimes beyond. Most further education institutions have their own disciplinary procedures and prefer these to be used instead of invoking the criminal law. If the police do become involved, an offer by the institution to deal directly with the matter may often be acceptable. By contrast, for many young people these types of protective arrangement from late adolescence into early adulthood do not exist.

An important aspect of education beyond the minimum school-leaving age is the link it provides to future employment and career prospects. For the undergraduate, achievement of a good degree and taking a full part in the life of the institution increase career choices. But for many young people the situation is starkly different. The opportunities for apprenticeships or for steady work on leaving school at the age of sixteen have become scarce. The prospects for work of any kind, even 'dead end' jobs are bleak. In some parts of Britain more than six out of every ten school-leavers face the void of unemployment. While there is no proven clear-cut relationship between unemployment and crime, the status of joblessness leaves the young person more vulnerable to sentence to the prison system. As Norman Tutt has suggested, with high levels of youth unemployment the inclination is no longer for the state to encourage the development of young people but to guarantee their control (Tutt, 1984, p. 306).

The spectre of long-term unemployment casts its shadow beyond those immediately affected. The absence of work prospects for young people has especially insidious conse-quences for the home and school, sapping their effectiveness as developmental institutions.

The remainder of this chapter explores three applications of the developmental approach within the criminal justice process. First, the crucial gatekeeping role of the police is examined both in terms of its success in diverting young people away from criminal justice and also as a warning of how formalized schemes can have results very different from those intended. The two other examples explore attempts to identify and use resources in the community in managing young people and crime. Everthorpe borstal, as it then was, exemplifies the constraints inherent in efforts to link the incarcerative institution with the localities to which young people will be returning. Finally, the Woodlands Centre in Basingstoke provides rare testimony to what the term 'com-munity-based' might mean.

Policeman at the Gate

Many events and situations concerning young people which are brought to the attention of the police proceed no further, because police officers decide that prosecution would serve no useful purpose. Traditionally this takes the form of an informal warning. The proverbial 'clip round the ear' and 'cuffing' (noting the offender's name in the officer's shirt cuff) means there is no further progress into the criminal justice process. As one chief constable has observed: 'Officers regard street cautions as part of the normal learning process of young persons' (Laugharne, 1983). On an informal basis, cautioning was a way out of the criminal justice process. It was when some cautions were made on a formal basis that the problems began.

Following endorsement of the notion of 'diversion' in the white paper of 1968 *Children in Trouble* and in the Children and Young Persons Act 1969, many police forces greatly increased the number of juveniles they formally cautioned. Prior to the 1969 Act one third of 10–13 year olds and one fifth of 14–16 year olds were formally cautioned. By 1983 more than three quarters of 10–13 year olds and about half the older group were cautioned. On the other hand, only 4 per cent of young adults were cautioned.* Decisions not to prosecute are determined in part by the assessment by the police of the young person's attitude and social circumstances. The Home Office has referred to 'parental attitude: the ability and willingness of the offender's parent or guardian to help the offender take heed of the caution' (Home Office, 1984*b*, p. 29). Trevor Bennett has examined the impact of parents' attitudes on the decision by police about prosecution. He quotes two contrasting police reports. One assessment reads: 'The television was on all the time I was speaking

* These percentages are of the number of young people cautioned out of the total found guilty or formally cautioned for indictable offences.

to Mr X and, though on two separate occasions I asked him to turn it off, he merely turned it fractionally down.' And, with reference to the daughter of a building-society manager: 'They are intelligent, well-oriented parents and have kept the incident in its true perspective; that is against her normal rational outlook.' Bennett found that 'not only do working-class parents seem to praise their children far less than middle-class parents in the presence of the juvenile bureau officer, but also they frequently seem to offer quite damaging information very likely to enhance the juvenile's delinquent identity'. One middle-class parent, by contrast, produced a character reference written by the local vicar (Bennett, 1979, pp. 142–4). In reviewing explanations for the lower use of cautions of black youngsters, a different London study found that black juveniles more frequently came from disrupted families than did their white counterparts. The authors comment: 'These conditions may also reduce the likelihood of full co-operation between the juvenile's parents and the juvenile bureau' (Landau and Nathan, 1983, p. 144). Decisions on whether or not to prosecute may also be influenced by the school and by social services departments. On some occasions, social services seek prosecution as a short-cut to obtaining a care order.

By the early 1970s the American diversion experience should have been a powerful warning to policy-makers that as police cautioning became formalized the likely result would be not to narrow but to widen the criminal justice net. The danger was twofold. First, in addition to replacing prosecution as intended, formal cautioning would also replace some informal cautions. The Home Office guide to the 1969 Act reminded police officers that informal warnings and taking no further action remained important alternatives to prosecution. Nine years later the Home Office reminded chief police officers that formal cautions required sufficient evidence to prosecution and an admission of guilt by the juvenile in the presence of parents. The second net-widening danger was that the formal caution would have consequences similar to those of conviction. This would be the result if formal cautions became part of any subsequent court proceedings. By the mid-1970s it was clear that this was the practice of many courts, and in 1978 it was endorsed by the Home Office. An allied danger is that cautioning results in informal supervision or some other programme placement. Diversion into programmes typified much of the American scene and exacerbated net-widening results. Some Intermediate Treatment projects have used police cautioning schemes as a means of recruiting clients, and in such instances net-widening can only result. Some research findings have underlined the danger of net-widening resulting from formal cautions. David Steer found that in two out of every five cautions there was either insufficient evidence for caution or the complainant was unwilling to give evidence (Steer, 1970). The impact of formal cautioning in London was examined by Farrington and Bennett, who concluded that there was a widening of the net of arrested juveniles especially in the younger, under-fourteen age group (Farrington and Bennett, 1981, p. 128).

The diversionary effect of the caution increases if police are encouraged to re-caution young people. These are cases where the court would probably be less inclined to consider a lenient disposal. A recent study found that eight police forces explicitly permitted second cautions, and these included forces with the highest cautioning rates. In Suffolk, for example, where 28 per cent of repeaters were cautioned, the standing orders read: 'proceedings will normally be taken if the juvenile has been formally cautioned on two separate occasions or has made a court appearance for a similar offence' (Laycock and Tarling, 1984, p. 39).

The formal cautioning rate for young adults by most police area forces has remained very low. In 1982 only three forces had rates above 10 per cent. Greater use of formal cautions for this age group seems likely to receive more official support.* It is now official practice that any record of adult, including young adult, cautions be available in any subsequent court proceeding.

Everthorpe

The incarcerative institution faces insuperable obstacles in any serious pursuit of the developmental approach. This proposition was amply confirmed during the early 1970s at Everthorpe borstal where attempts were made to bring about organizational changes which would make the institution relevant to the situation facing the young men on their release. Everthorpe, which is now a 'youth custody centre', is a secure institution, holding about 300 'trainees' aged between fifteen and nineteen. The institution is situated in a rural part of East Yorkshire, about 150 miles from where many of the trainees live. Certainly in the early 1970s most of the trainees were from the industrial areas of Merseyside and Manchester.

Over a three-year period efforts were made by staff and trainees to bring about changes within the institution and in relation to the mandatory period of supervision following release. The results were clear-cut. No substantial change was achieved within the institution, but some significant steps were taken to alter the after-care relationship between trainee and probation officer. By 1972 the conclusion was evident: 'We are in need of some form of declaration that states our work is within the urban setting' (Rutherford, 1973).

The organizational tool selected to bring about the required

---

* Recommendations to this effect were made by the All Party Parliamentary Penal Affairs Group (1981) and a Home Office working party (Home Office, 1984).

change was the 'workshop'. One or two full-day sessions involving trainees and staff focused on offending patterns and particular types of crime. Increasingly, people were invited to workshops from the trainees' home localities. Such persons included former trainees, police officers, magistrates and probation officers. Frequently, trainees would ask that members of the local CID be invited and, despite the distances, occasionally the invitations were accepted. The ensuing discussions focused on mutual stereotypes and the task of the former borstal trainee in convincing the local police that he was staying out of trouble. The positive response by the police highlighted the potential within police forces to recognize the support required for young people with serious criminal records.

One of the most regular events was the after-care workshop which drew its participants from a particular town or city in northern England and generally involved six to ten probation officers, around twenty trainees and several borstal staff. The after-care workshop was especially conducive to spill-over or what Douglas and Joan Grant once called 'the principle of contagion'. This spill-over mainly took the form of after-care groups involving one probation officer and up to eight trainees from the same area. While the trainees were in the borstal the probation officer visited and met with the group every two or three weeks and continued to meet regularly after release. The group setting provided mutual support and allowed for a greater degree of negotiation between probation officer and former trainee than would be likely with one-to-one supervision. For example, a group might agree to meet away from the probation office. Agreement sometimes was made to involve others such as girlfriends and family members. After-care groups directly challenged the long-established assumption that ex-offenders should be kept apart.

About half of the groups established inside continued to function after discharge. A Teesside probation officer wrote:

The after-care group is part of a scheme which is ambitious yet experimental. It would be premature to suggest any firm conclusions and the significant test of the group's work and viability is still to come. The project does not imply rejection of traditional probationary techniques which are still applicable to the majority of our clients. It is geared specifically to borstal trainees from a common home area. If the group disintegrated tomorrow I would feel that efforts thus far were worthwhile in view of the extent of discussion and the fact that a willingness to consider alternatives has been generated. I am fairly hopeful that the group will survive in Teesside. It will be a considerable time before we can assess the impact, if any, on reconviction rates. Nevertheless the experience of the last seven months would seem to justify an enthusiastic continuation of the experiment. (Keane, 1972)

Another group which was based on the vast housing conurbation of Kirkby near Liverpool was also described by its probation officer:

After twelve months' existence it seems appropriate to review the process by which the group started and the progress it has made. In crude statistical terms the group has been very successful. Six months after release all four members still had their liberty and three of the four are still in work. Only one offence has been committed, that of under-age drinking by the member who lost his job. The group has provided its members with an opportunity for dynamic growth. Group pressures have been strong and have been given as one reason for avoiding delinquent involvement. Each of the members has verbalized his intention of not being the first to break down. It has also been interesting to note the development of individuals within the group. One individual has assumed a dominant role, both economically and emotionally, in his fatherless family. Another, initially introverted and withdrawn with his problems compounded by a bad stutter, has now gained sufficient self confidence to be a successful operator as a door to door salesman.

In attempting to assess the success of this group the probation officer noted that contributory factors may well have been the fact they were released on the same date, that there had been a large number of meetings within the borstal prior to release, and that the small size of the group itself may in some ways have been useful. He feels that a further factor was his own personal commitment to the group and a heavy investment of his time and effort. This, he says, certainly affected his attitude towards the group on release. He wrote that he learned something of the sociological and psychological factors that foster criminal behaviour. 'Perhaps the biggest single factor I have noted that seems to have affected the attitude and behaviour of the group is that of maturation'; and he continued: 'now the lads can buy clothes and entertainment, visit clubs and stay out late, they no longer feel the need to steal.' He added:

This is perhaps a none too startling conclusion after twelve months' hard work, however, it was important for me to learn this and for the group to see I had learned, in fact the group members have demanded part of my salary as they consider I have done nothing to modify their attitudes and behaviour. They see it very much as coming from within themselves as a process of maturation. However, they are willing to admit that I was able to retain a focus on this developmental process and this is perhaps the significance of the Kirkby After-Care group. (Whiffin, 1972)

Several key lessons emerge from the Everthorpe experience. In the first place, the institution was very much more resilient to change than external agencies such as the probation service. Although many borstal staff demonstrated considerable enthusiasm, the demands of the custodial organization limited the contribution they were able to make. On the other hand, probation officers displayed considerable adaptability. Their involvement in workshops and after-care groups appeared to give them greater confidence in being able to hold young persons in the community. There was, for example, a greater expressed willingness to avoid recommendations for custody in writing social inquiry reports to courts.

135

This new confidence also applied to the trainees, who demonstrated commitment and skills in keeping themselves and others out of incarcerative institutions.

Of primary importance, the Everthorpe experience strongly suggested that the institutional part of the borstal sentence might be dispensed with. The incarcerative institution got in the way of and postponed the critical work which had to be done. In other words, for sentencers and probation departments the implication was that the required resources actually existed to bypass the institutional stage. What was needed was the means by which these resources might be harnessed. From the borstal setting it was not possible to reach out sufficiently to persons and groups outside the criminal justice system. Spill-over from the institution into the localities of the young people clearly has much less potential for bringing about change than efforts firmly rooted in the community.

The Woodlands Centre

In the summer of 1981 several citizens of Basingstoke, a town in north Hampshire with a population of about 132,000, took innovative steps to deal with young people and crime. There was growing despair that the juvenile court did not have local alternatives to incarcerative institutions, and a powerful determination emerged to do something about it. The main initiative was taken by Margaret Baring, chairperson of the juvenile court. She and other magistrates, the clerk to the court and other local people wanted a programme which did more than pack young people and canoes into a mini-bus.

Baring was able to interest the Rainer Foundation in her ideas. Named after Frederick Rainer, a Hertfordshire printer who gave a few shillings to the Church of England Temperance Society to undertake missionary work in police courts, the Rainer Foundation was founded in 1876. With its considerable experience in responding to young people in trouble, the Rainer Foundation in the early 1980s gave priority to initiating a variety of community-based programmes. In assuming responsibility for the Woodlands Centre, the Foundation acquired the necessary funding and appointed the first director.

The arrival of Chris Green at the Woodlands Centre determined that the programme's sights were set on Basingstoke rather than on the criminal justice arena. Green had been a member of a research team at Lancaster University which served as a resource to local authorities wishing to develop alternatives to sentences of care and custody. He brought much more than concern for programme ideas to the new project; he insisted that Woodlands should be as much concerned with changing the existing pattern of decision-making across juvenile justice, especially with reference to sentencing. A unique feature of the Basingstoke initiative was the recognition that, unless process issues were addressed, programme aspects might be counter-productive. Under Green's direction, Woodlands was to deal with older adolescents (not the younger age group who were in the minds of some of the founder group), and to confine its attention to young people who almost certainly would otherwise receive institutional sentences. Green firmly rejected the conventional interpretation of Intermediate Treatment, or IT as it had become known. The 1968 white paper *Children in Trouble* had called for a new legal and administrative framework which would encourage 'the development of a variety of forms of intermediate treatment for children placed under supervision by the courts'. The white paper also envisaged that IT would be used as a preventive measure for young persons who had not been before the courts. During the 1970s most IT programmes remained firmly located at the periphery of the criminal justice process. Indeed, not infrequently, IT projects were located outside the criminal process, dealing with youngsters deemed to be at risk not of custody, but of crime. The proliferation of IT activities occurred with disregard to the effect on decision-making within criminal-justice. The result was that not only did IT fail to reduce sentences to the prison system, but it widened the net by bringing young people into the criminal justice process. The American experience, which contained profound warnings, was either unknown or ignored. Most social workers were too busy to find time for reading. By contrast, the Woodlands Centre adamantly refused to paddle safely in the 'shallow end' and opted for the tougher challenges of the 'deep end'. According to Green, Woodlands had 'the uncompromising objective of reducing the number of custodial and residential sentences in the juvenile court to zero' (Green, 1983a). Green was confident that the courts could be provided with an alternative to incarceration in which they had confidence. The Woodlands Centre also saw as its mandate

to develop a response to crime and delinquency which focuses upon the offence and the damage done, which is rigorous and constructive – and which thus seeks to minimise the damage done by the juvenile's offence, both to the community and within the lives of the young offenders themselves; to reduce the incidence of re-offending by juveniles, and nurture growth into a mature and law abiding adulthood. (Green, 1983a)

Woodlands is a two-storey structure situated on a housing estate within Basingstoke. The Centre operates during weekday evenings, mostly providing a one-to-one focus on the pattern and circumstances of offending and consideration of alternatives. Aims of the programme are:

- To identify rational behaviour responsible for the offences, which might then be modified to produce behavioural changes.
- To reidentify the young person with his or her immediate locality, and to build trust and shared relationships

between young people and the community so that the individual can undertake some form of reparation for the offences committed.

- To confront the young person with issues of responsibility and control.
- To detail a process of reconciliation between the individual and the community. By involving the young person in community issues, the community may abandon stereotypes about the young person.

Chris Green and his colleagues explicitly recognize how much their approach contrasts with that of the incarcerative institution. Removing the young person from his or her locality is 'to remove him or her from the scene of the offence and any subsequent responsibility for reparation and atonement'. The result of incarceration is mutual isolation and labelling: 'This isolation and labelling of young offenders from community members results in two groups having little or no contact with each other' (Green, 1983*b*). For Woodlands the targets of change are both the young person and the locality.

The Woodlands Centre combines an informal atmosphere with firm and clearly articulated requirements of the young people it serves. While the shape of the programme continues to evolve and develop, the overall intent is to provide for different levels of intervention according to seriousness of offence and offending pattern. The 'high intensity' programme is intended as an alternative to sentences of youth custody. This consists of 280 hours of attendance over a period of twelve months. As attendance is reduced the focus is widened to include social problems and difficulties in general. During this stage youngsters may carry out studies of offending patterns or examine particular problems such as youth unemployment or glue-sniffing.

For young people who would otherwise have received care orders or detention centre sentences, a 'medium intensity' programme consists of 100 hours of attendance over a period of six months and a condensed version of the programme undertaken by the high-intensity group. The third group is a spill-over from the early months of the Centre's existence and was not originally anticipated. During this time there were several referrals for whom full programmes would have been inappropriate, either because of the minor nature of their offences (which would warrant rather lower tariff sentences such as fines or supervision orders) or because of the limited extent of their criminal careers to date. It was thought that for this group, particularly those in the latter category, a confrontational focus on offences and offending might confirm rather than reduce their commitment to delinquency; so the Centre offered voluntary attendance for the Thursday night activities with the addition of some weekly reporting or contact sessions with the Woodlands staff. These youngsters were not subject to Intermediate Treatment orders, and their attendance was arranged in conjunction with social workers or probation officers. The final group are youngsters who wish to participate in recreational and social activities. Most of these are friends or acquaintances of others who already attend the Centre. For one evening each week Woodlands serves to enhance local youth club provision.

Woodlands is pioneering a variety of novel ways of working with young people. One important technique is to have the young people draw cartoons of their offences and offending patterns as a means of identifying trigger points.

Burglary of a warehouse (cartoon overleaf)

Note provided by Woodlands staff:

This cartoon was completed by a fifteen-year-old; it was his first offence, and he got involved with a group of young lads who acquired keys to the warehouse through an earlier burglary. Originally the idea was only to do the warehouse once, but having easily got away with it the first time they met again in the Chang Hoo and agreed to do it a second time (cartoon episode 6). The author of the cartoon was quick to see the escalation in his offending and the temptation to take part. For each cartoon he provided points at which he could have backed out of the offence and said no.

Young people at Woodlands are also involved in role plays focusing on their offences. These may be put on video so that the group can then discuss the content of the role play. Photography is used to trace the young person's life history by setting off with a camera into Basingstoke and its surrounds where photographs are taken of scenes illustrating the young person's life. A staff member has described how she was taken by a youngster to photograph the mental hospital where his mother was a patient for some years.

While the first six months of the programme are based at the Woodlands Centre, the final three months involve a community placement serving as a means of reparation for the offence, not to the individual victim but to the community as a whole. The placement is located near to where the offence took place and consists of working one evening a week, often with a youth group or tenants' association. A purpose of the placement is for the young person to become incorporated into a network of people which in turn provides friendship and support. Put another way, the placement serves to bind the young person into his or her locality.

The assistant director, Pauline Owen, has described the spill-over from community placements in a passage which captures the essence of the developmental approach:

It is within community placements that the most significant changes have occurred. Growing from a crude notion of using

1

'My friends and I met at the Chinese at 7.00 pm.'

2

'We decided to walk into town. On our way we walked past a warehouse. Two of my friends had the keys to it.'

3

'One of my friends suggested we go into the warehouse.'

Points where I could have said no and avoided getting involved:

1. I could have backed out by not turning up.
2. I could have walked to town a different way.
3. I could have said it was dangerous to go in.

'Inside there was lots of drink. We took some and left.'

'We drank some in the park and threw the rest away.
Then we went home.'

Next day: 'We met at about the same time the next day and decided
to go to the warehouse.'

4. Once inside I could have said I was scared and left.
5. I could have not drunk anything and said I didn't want anything
   to do with it.
6. I could have not turned up.

voluntary help and effecting indirect reparation, *the placements now encourage the local community to take an interest in, and indeed, 'manage' the delinquents within their area.* Obviously, this requires support, encouragement and supervision from the Centre, but we have been encouraged by the positive response shown by local communities in dealing with their young offenders. Through such local help, the youngster is encouraged to develop local ties within his/her immediate environment, and gain respect for work achieved. The community, on the other hand, benefits from the indirect reparation, and from the growth of a more mature and socially integrated young person. (Owen, 1984, emphasis added)

The impact of Woodlands on the local criminal justice process is of considerable significance. In 1980 eighteen juveniles were sentenced to the prison system. In 1982, the first operational year for Woodlands, there were five custodial sentences. In 1983 there were two. This remarkable transformation in sentencing practice was largely achieved as a result of the Woodlands Centre assuming a gatekeeping role at the point when a custodial sentence or an alternative disposition at that level of the tariff is being considered. In the period 1981–3 some thirty youngsters were received at Woodlands on orders from the court. Another fifteen to twenty were assessed by the programme. Remarkably, these youngsters were refused not because they were too difficult to handle but because their offences were not high enough on the tariff. That is to say, in the view of the Woodlands staff, the case did not merit a custodial sentence, and the young people were diverted to lower-tariff sentences. This gatekeeping function may have contributed to the reduction in the number of referrals to Woodlands after its second year of operation. For the gatekeeping role to be effective it is essential that potential cases are referred to the Centre. Once the department of social services or the probation service have received notification of prosecution by the police, and if care or custodial sentences are a possibility, arrangements are made for the Woodlands

Centre to make an assessment. The assessment consists of a minimum of two family interviews and two individual interviews with the young person. The assessment concentrates on the offence and the young person's offending pattern, forming the basis of the Centre's report to court. If an IT order specifying Woodlands is recommended, the report specifies what will be demanded of the young person. The report subsequently becomes the contract between Woodlands and the young person. As the requirements are demanding, the youngster must fully understand and be willing to comply with the order. In preparing a report to court the Woodlands staff anticipate that there is likely to be a future court appearance. A crucial feature of Woodlands is to hold on to young people, and any breach of the order, if the court is to be persuaded, would not result in removal to an incarcerative institution.

Although the Woodlands Centre is closely aligned to the court its approach bears little resemblance to the punishment approach; nor do notions of treatment and welfare provide a useful framework for assessing its contribution. Both in terms of the way it deals with young people and with reference to the impact on its locality, the work at Woodlands precedes the language by which it might be described. In programme terms, Woodlands is consistent with the developmental approach. Young people are held accountable for harm they have caused. A full assessment of the offence and its consequences connects with strategies to provide for atonement and reparation. The essence of the Woodlands programme is to bind the young person with the locality. In this respect, Woodlands has made little attempt to work with families. Family counselling is regarded as excessively time-consuming, and the Woodlands staff also doubt its appropriateness. It is felt that the involvement of families might shift responsibility for the offence away from the young person and, furthermore, that by the age of sixteen many young people are looking for support from beyond their families. The Woodlands Centre is used as families and schools might be used. Woodlands is pioneering the developmental approach by seeking to mobilize wider sources of support and control within the locality.

Woodlands has successfully brought about changes within the local criminal justice process. In particular, fewer young people have been sentenced to the prison system. This is an especially remarkable achievement given the new short detention centre provisions which took effect in May 1983. The minimum three-week sentence to detention centre, with one week off for good behaviour, has eroded the threshold between custody and alternative sanctions. In 1984 six juveniles received custodial sentences in Basingstoke. Two of these were for twenty-one days and a further three for twenty-eight days. The disturbing implications of the new sentencing provisions remain to be worked out by Woodlands staff in conjunction with local criminal justice practitioners.

Consistent with the developmental approach, the Woodlands Centre has experienced continual adaptation and innovation. Furthermore, the Centre's excellent relations with the police, probation service and other agencies is evidenced in useful spill-over. Examples include a senior police officer's considering using unemployed young people as car park attendants in order to discourage theft, and the local probation service's application of the Centre's approach to young adults. The Woodlands staff are anxious that the Centre's physical location does not inhibit it from being more fully absorbed by the town.

The impact of Woodlands reaches beyond local criminal justice arrangements. An essential task of the Centre is to use its knowledge and experience of young people and crime to benefit the local community. Advice on crime prevention has been packaged and distributed to households; information on the use made of recreational facilities in the town centre has been submitted to the town council; and exploratory work has been carried out to set up a victim support group. Pauline Owen has aptly described the Centre's role as 'providing both information and skill in managing delinquency within Basingstoke and providing information valuable to the work of crime prevention' (Owen, 1984).

Chapter Five

Danger Ahead

In this era of economic difficulty, we can expect more social junk to be washed upon the shores of economic decline, and more entrepreneurs to seek a living from their bodies. Juvenile delinquents, the elderly, the nonworking, and other socially useless persons, the mentally ill, the mentally retarded, the handicapped, the sick and the criminal – all are potential sources of revenue from these new and other, still newer, forms of social control. (Carol Warren, 1981, p. 739)

•

Warning signs are all too easily disregarded. In 1975 an American sociologist, Paul Lerman, clearly spelled out the unintended and unanticipated consequences of some criminal justice reforms. He demonstrated, for example, that the much-heralded probation subsidy scheme in California had not reduced incarceration but had shifted its locus from state to local government (Lerman, 1975). In 1982 Lerman was again the bearer of bad tidings. Commenting on efforts to remove young people from penal institutions across the United States, he suggested that many were now held in other types of institution (Lerman, 1982). The following year Krisberg and Schwartz reported that a private institutional system had rapidly evolved for disruptive or 'acting out' young people who are no longer processed by the public juvenile control agencies (Krisberg and Schwartz, 1983; see also Austin and Krisberg, 1982). The appearance of new

Unattributed quotations are from the BBC radio documentary *The Child Fixers*, first broadcast on 18 October 1984.

148

forms of incarceration has led some scholars to dismiss decarceration as an illusion. Instead of there being less reliance on institutions, they suggest there has been a shift of young people from one type of institution to another or 'transinstitutionalism', representing a shift from criminal justice to mental health and also from public to private social control. One girl's experience illustrates some of the forces at work.

The trouble with Sarah was that she was a punk rocker and had rather more rows with her parents than most girls of her age. Furthermore, her father, a prominent American educator, was exasperated by fifteen-year-old Sarah's apparent lack of ambition. A psychiatrist recommended that Sarah be examined at a hospital in Minnesota, some 1,500 miles away, with a view to in-patient treatment. Sarah was told that she was going to Minnesota with her parents for educational tests. On reaching the hospital Sarah refused to get out of the car, and she was forcibly taken into the building by hospital employees. The clinical staff decided, with her parents' agreement, that Sarah should be admitted to the hospital. Eleven months later, Sarah contacted a Minneapolis lawyer who later recalled:

> She was a punk rocker. She smoked heavily but she did not use drugs or alcohol. I think to her credit she had successfully avoided becoming involved with the kind of life-style to keep her out overnight and that would get involved with drug use. She said in an insightful way that she was a teenager, an adolescent, and she simply needed time to work that through. At one point she said to me, 'I understand that I'm not going to be involved with punk rock for my entire life but it's a phase and I should be allowed to go through it, shouldn't I.'

After meeting Sarah, the lawyer wrote to the hospital director. The letter stated that Sarah 'is not mentally ill, yet she has been admitted and retained against her will without

149

even a neutral independent psychiatric examination directed to determining whether she needs prolonged treatment . . . Although we have advised our client that there is a basis for litigation, we believe it is important to make the attempt to resolve the issue by means of negotiation.' Sarah was promptly released and she returned home. The hospital fees, at $350 per day, amounted to about $120,000 and these were paid by her parents' private health insurance.

Sarah's experience testifies to the rapidly expanding practice of placing children, some as young as two years old, in private psychiatric hospitals across the United States and mostly paid for by insurance premiums. In Minnesota, for example, the admission rate of children to psychiatric hospitals, situated in the major metropolitan area, more than doubled between 1976 and 1983; over the same period the rate of admissions across the state of juveniles (persons up to the age of eighteen) for in-patient psychiatric treatment increased from 91 to 184 per 100,000 of that age group. In 1982 the average length of stay for juveniles was thirty-eight days compared with twenty-one days for adults. Data from Blue Shield and Blue Cross, a major non-profit private health insurance company, show that 'admissions are most often made for emotional disturbance, conduct disorder, neurotic disorder, depression and adjustment reaction' (Schwartz et al., 1984, p. 37). As a proportion of insured cases, juveniles rose from 16 to 24 per cent between 1978 and 1982.

The new industry has expanded at an extraordinary pace, with most of the growth taking place since the early 1970s. The main driving force is economics. The context has been bluntly described by one observer: 'the policy of deinstitutionalization is best understood as a political and economic measure designed to sustain near-bankrupt state governments and to establish the basis for transferring funds from public services to the private sector' (Rose, 1979, pp. 444–5). In the early 1970s there was considerable concern in Minnesota about the lack of care for the mentally ill and for 'chemically dependent' persons abusing alcohol and drugs. With the state's tradition of high-quality health care it was hardly surprising that Minnesota became the first state to mandate legislatively that private health insurance include coverage for psychiatric and chemical dependency treatment. Insurance is now playing the crucial role. As noted by a citizens' organization:

Having had favourable experiences with employees treated at Hazeldon and other centres, Minnesota corporations began including chemical dependency treatment in their employee health packages. Such coverage expanded voluntarily during the late 1960s and early 1970s. In 1973, the Minnesota legislature required health insurance plans to cover chemical dependency treatment in hospitals. The results of the interlocking relationship between insurance companies and treatment centres is disturbing, the system of funding for chemical dependency treatment in large part determined the type of treatment which often was the most expensive and intensive treatment available. (Citizens League, 1984)

Legislatures acted with the best of intentions but failed to pay heed to the vulnerable status of young people. For health care companies such legislation has been highly opportune. Hospital care in the United States has been going through difficult times, largely as the result of an over-capacity of hospital beds. The wider insurance coverage of mental health and chemical dependency has enabled health care companies, in the words of one executive, 'to reposition themselves in the market place'. Companies have transferred their activities from relatively unprofitable areas such as medical surgery, where insurers insist that diagnostic categories limit in-patient days, to the more lucrative pastures of behavioural medicine where no such limits exist. The daily fee is unlikely to be less than $200 and at one hospital in California exceeds $1,000. Surgical wards are being closed to make way for locked wards, very often for adolescents. One health care company spokesperson explained: 'In 1983, we closed those units where we had medical surgery problems, coronary care and intensive care. We believe that our speciality areas are mental health and chemical dependency treatment.' The hospital chief administrator had this to say:

Well, obviously to remain viable you have to be able to produce a bottom line, a profit, and a lot of institutions across the United States are going out of business because they cannot produce a bottom line. They are going to look down at their services and they are going to say, 'We can make money around the behavioural medicine', but they don't necessarily make money on open heart or cardiac surgery or some of the other kinds of speciality work.

A report by the Metropolitan Health Board of Minnesota confirmed this trend, showing that during the 1970s in-patient hospital utilization rates declined significantly. Medical and surgical hospital usage rates fell from 902 days per 1,000 in 1970 to 774 in 1980. The rates for pediatric hospitals fell from 108 to 65 days and for obstetric hospitals from 87 to 69. By contrast, in-patient chemical dependency rates rose from 57 to 73 days and psychiatric rates from 103 to 127. A Minnesota citizens' group commented in 1984: 'These trends lead some health policy analysts to wonder whether hospitals were using these services to fill empty beds' (Citizens' League, 1984). Blue Cross and Blue Shield of Minnesota have reported that juvenile psychiatric in-patient claims between 1978 and 1982 increased at more than twice the rate for adults. As Patricia Guttridge and Carol Warren of the University of Southern California have commented, in theory any expansion of entitlements through insurance should serve to protect individuals from social control but this is not the case for young people 'volunteered' into hospitals by their parents.

The shift in hospital bed-space is accompanied by extensive marketing activity. Advertising on television and radio is targeted with precision. One health company official commenting on the choice of programmes for their television advertisements remarked: 'We advertise on all of the channels but we advertise on certain shows because our marketing is for a certain social class. So, one of the programs that we advertise on is the *Rockford Files*.' Asked if the target audience is predominantly middle class, the official replied, 'Certainly, white middle-class America.'

One advertisement has this to say to parents: 'What will your child be taking in school this year? You are convinced he is using drugs, and drinking too. He's had trouble in school and scrapes with the law. No parent wants to admit that his child is in such serious trouble, but you are at the end of your rope . . . Call the Adolescent Care Unit. No one ever said growing up was easy.' The same firm informs hospitals that they may be missing 'an opportunity to put under-utilized beds to profitable use . . . Better than 95 per cent of the nation's alcoholics are middle class, successful and responsible citizens. The Care Unit program caters to precisely these kind of people.' In its advertising to recruit staff for 'adolescent chemical dependency opportunities', another company in Texas states that the 'candidates will have previous experience in all phases of adolescent chemical dependency treatment and possess strong marketing and management skills.'

The marketing strategy includes 'outreach' into schools. Health company officials explain to teachers what their psychiatric facility has to offer. Troublesome children, given the agreement of parents, can, at least for the time being, be removed. A health care marketing specialist, formerly a child therapist, has explained that she visited primary and secondary schools offering 'a way out' with pupils that teachers cannot manage in class:

We also offer them a free service where we will come out to do a free evaluation. There are some teachers in the schools who believe that you should keep children out of the hospital almost under any circumstances. I really work at trying to convince them that we are not trying to get business that we don't need to have, but we are trying to get the business of kids who really need to be hospitalized.

She went on to relate the case of a fifteen-year-old boy who had been referred by a teacher:

I met with the child and I met with the father, and the child was clearly psychotic and needed to be intervened with some medication. The school people told me that he had been in and out of psychosis for the past five years. He was in and out of reality, with beliefs that he was going to be a football star . . . but he was a very small-built child, not athletic in any shape or form.

Having made the diagnosis, she admitted the boy to the hospital and two days later a psychiatrist confirmed her opinion 'and put him on some medication which clearly helped him'. She was asked whether the boy's parents wanted him to be hospitalized:

A: I believe there was some fear. It was helpful for them to see someone that didn't look like I was going to lock him up.
Q: But you were going to lock him up weren't you?
A; No, well he is in the hospital so he is locked up but it is different than being in a jail; they can't leave the grounds, that is true.

Teachers are regarded as an especially valuable referral source and are regularly invited to special events at the hospital. For psychiatrists, the relationship with the hospital may be rather closer. One hospital has an accreditation process whereby the psychiatrists who make referrals are hired to make consulting visits to the hospital for a weekly fee of $300 per visited patient. 'It is a 50/50 relationship, we give them as much business as they give us, 'a health care company executive explained. As Carol Warren found in her California study, there are large profits to be made not only for the hospital-owners but for others involved. At least one hospital-owner is considering setting up an insurance company to address directly the client group in which he is a specialist.

For parents, as for teachers, the health care industry offers the seductive promise of a quick fix. Parents become convinced that there is an institutional panacea for difficulties within the school and the family. Instead of making additional efforts to keep the child in the home and school, market forces favour in-patient intervention. A study by the Health Insurance Association of America found that most policies covered less that $1,500 per year for out-patient psychiatric care, while in-patient psychiatric care was covered at the same level as other medical problems. Some parents fail to appreciate the long-term consequences of their child having a record of in-patient psychiatric care. Furthermore, parents may be reluctant to disagree with medical professionals or to question the validity of treatment terminology. Youngsters are being admitted to psychiatric facilities under an array of 'conduct disorders'. In a study of four hospitals in the Los Angeles area, Guttridge and Warren found that 70 per cent of adolescent admissions were for anti-social behaviour, depression, running away, drug abuse or personality disorders. 'Hospital staff routinely divide their adolescent patients into those with nothing really wrong with them other than behaviour problems and the "really mentally ill".' Diagnoses include 'adolescent adjustment reaction' and 'attention deficit disorder' (Guttridge and Warren, 1984).

Vague diagnostic criteria, the availability of insurance coverage and aggressive marketing have continued to produce what Minnesota state representative Connie Levi calls 'third-party-payment-driven diagnosis'. In other words, the condition which justifies admission is determined by what is reimbursable under insurance coverage. One law enforcement official has been quoted as saying: 'A decade ago, kids with problems were sent off to boarding-schools. Now they're being sent to psychiatric hospitals as so-called voluntary patients. This is a real problem, and the public policy-makers in California have not been able to deal with it.' Or, as stated by an academic lawyer: 'By and large, kids are being hospitalized as much for the parents as for the kids. It's an easier solution to put the kid in the hospital than deal with the family system or deal with the child in the home.'* Warren and Guttridge conclude: 'A lot of these kids are your basic Southern California adolescent.' Seventy per cent of the Los Angeles admissions were for anti-social behaviour, personality disorders, depression or running away from home. Warren observed: 'Parents may want to avoid routine parental duties or gain respite from the troublesome child.' The middle-class young person has suddenly become vulnerable. 'If middle-class parents are bothered by their adolescent's behaviour, they have both the resources (financial, through insurance policies and/or fees) and the power (of legal and medical decision-making over the adolescent) to hospitalize the minor. The middle-class youngster is more liable to "voluntary" incarceration than the lower-class adolescent' (Guttridge and Warren, 1984). As put by a legal commentator: 'the child whose parents can afford to pay for his institutionalization has less protection than his poorer counterpart.' With the length of stay as the measure, the higher the social class the longer the average stay (Dillon et al., 1982, p. 21).

An official report in California found: 'In family crisis situations, it is often the middle-class parent who is unable to manage what might appear as normal adolescent behaviour of the acting out kind . . . in these cases, there is no real severe pathology, but the family is unable to cope . . . in many cases it is the family (the parent) who is in crisis and not the child' (Orange County Board of Supervisors Report, 1980, p. 8, cited in Guttridge and Warren, 1984). One hospital

* Stephen Morse quoted in the *Los Angeles Times*, 14 August 1983.

counsellor acknowledged that 'almost always you find that it is a family issue; it is not just the patient who has got the problem'. The following dialogue ensued:

Q: But it is the child who is being treated as the patient.

A: Right, that's true.

Q: It seems unfair, doesn't it?

A: Well sometimes there needs to be an identified patient before something can be initiated.

There are few protections for children against inappropriate admission to a psychiatric hospital where they may be subject to physical treatments. The United States Supreme Court in *Parham v-J.R.* (1979) overturned decisions by lower courts to hold that: 'Most children, even in adolescence, simply are not able to make sound judgments concerning many decisions, including their need for medical care and treatment. Parents can, and must, make these decisions.' The Supreme Court held that admission of a child to a psychiatric facility did not require a formal or even quasi-formal hearing but merely 'some kind of enquiry'. The law has not kept pace with the rapid growth of the problem. One legal commentator noted just prior to the *Parham* decision:

courts and legislatures have been left without guidance concerning the constitutionally acceptable alternatives to unfettered parental discretion . . . protecting the family from outside interference is quite distinct from fortifying the family's power over one of its members. Although constitutional support for the former is clear and well-established, the constitutional support for the latter is not.

The commentator held that by the age of fourteen the young person has acquired a basic capacity to make intelligent choices and that by this age the welfare rationale for parental authority loses most of its force (Note, 1978, pp. 187–202).

In theory the psychiatrist, with ultimate authority to accept or reject the commitment, should be a check on parental

157

autonomy. But as has been noted: 'in practice, there are many variations on this basic framework. Not only parents but juvenile authorities, schools, social workers, and other social institutions bring children with problems to the attention of mental health professionals' (Dillon et al., 1982, p. 385). But when mental health professionals err, there is a strong tendency to err on the side of over-diagnosis and, 'given the severe deprivation of liberty that accompanies involuntary commitment to a mental institution, many courts and commentators have concluded that if, on the request of parents, medical professionals have the sole authority to accept or reject commitments, the error rate will be constitutionally intolerable' (Dillon et al., 1982, p. 391).

Although designated as hospitals, the institutional settings share many security and control features with punishment institutions. Locked rooms, high-fenced recreational areas and other security paraphernalia abound. Similarly, there are pervasive concerns about control. At one hospital, on a unit of up to twenty children aged from two to thirteen, behind heavy locked doors there are three 'quiet rooms'. The senior counsellor explained:

> This room is called the quiet room. It is mostly used when patients need to take time out to express anger. We encourage them to look at it for more appropriate ways to deal with their anger. We may give them a ball to bounce on the walls, or a phone book to rip up.

She then pointed to a large mat, about one and a half inches thick.

> This mat you see on the floor is something that we may roll them up in to help them get in control. You lay them this way with their head at the top and you roll this across their body, and keep rolling them with their arms down at their side . . . the quiet room is a place where they are more free to express themselves, where they are not going to hurt themselves, or someone else.

Other forms of physical restraints and medication are used in many of these settings. Most of this 'treatment' remains out of sight of official regulatory agencies. The emerging privately administered and financed psychiatric control of young people remains largely unregulated by public agencies. This is especially likely to be the case where public funding is not involved. Guttridge and Warren comment: 'if mental hospitals are private and do not receive federal, county, state or local funds, then their in-patient censuses need not be reported to statistics-collecting public agencies.' They go on to comment: 'Public funds are avoided to remain free from both reporting requirements and accounting strings attached to public monies' (Guttridge and Warren, 1984; see also Warren, 1984).

In Minnesota, for example, officials in state regulatory departments of health and social services do not know how many young people are held in private psychiatric hospital settings. Ira Schwartz of the Hubert H. Humphrey Institute of Public Affairs at the University of Minnesota has aptly written of the new 'hidden' system of juvenile control (Schwartz et al., 1984). State government in Minnesota is only just beginning to grapple with the implications for public policy of the hidden system. The non-partisan Citizens League has voiced concerns, and a state-wide task force has been set up; but it remains doubtful that there will be effective public regulation of what has become a highly profitable industry. Since 1981 Blue Cross and Blue Shield of Minnesota have been screening cases, but only after treatment has been completed. No such screening is carried out by commercial insurers which account for almost two thirds of the private insurance market.

Although direct comparisons are difficult to make, there are some disturbing similarities between Britain in the mid-1980s and Minnesota in the early 1970s. There are about 10,000 private hospital beds in Britain, but the occupancy rate is estimated to be about 65 per cent. About 10 per cent of these beds are psychiatric. Private health insurance is growing, and about 2 per cent of in-patient claims are for psychiatric care. Of these claims, it has been estimated by BUPA that about 150 a year are for young persons under sixteen. There is also an expansion of privately administered residential settings, some of them locked, for young people with behavioural problems. These facilities mostly depend upon placements funded by local authorities and area health authorities. However, in one of these institutions, owned by a private health care company, a third of the residents are paid for through private health insurance. The American experience provides salutary warnings. In particular, Britain should be alerted to the flexible nature of boundaries between the public and private sector and across the arenas of criminal justice, welfare and mental health. Aspects of Samuel Butler's *Erewhon* are alive and well in Minnesota and other parts of the United States, and Ira Schwartz has made this warning to Britain: 'If you go down the path of what we have found out in Minnesota and also the rest of the country, you are going to be on the road of bankruptcy. It is going to cost an enormous amount of money; you will not be able to turn it around, and you're going to hurt a lot of kids and families in the process.'

There are some indications that in Britain the first steps have already been taken down the path described by Ira Schwartz and other observers of the American scene. Very few protections exist for young people under sixteen years old where parents seek 'voluntary' placement within mental health institutions. Rachel Hodgkin of the Children's Legal Centre has expressed alarm at the growth of the adolescent psychiatry industry in the United States, 'because we look to the States as having a better record on civil liberties than this country as America has a constitution which protects the individual's rights. What happens in America today may happen in this country tomorrow.' Indeed, American health

160

care companies are already advertising in British newspapers, with a particular focus on mental health problems and alcoholism. The increasing public concern regarding the misuse of heroin in Britain is likely to encourage private health care companies to broaden their marketing into the arena of narcotics and other drugs. As in the United States, government departments in Britain have shown little inclination to monitor closely the activities of private health care companies.

These events in Minnesota and throughout much of the United States demonstrate the extraordinary resilience of the treatment approach. The explosion in behavioural medicine with its wide and flexible net has brought new energy to the machinery of incarceration. The benign image of the hospital, which compares favourably with that of criminal justice and welfare institutions, is one source of this growth. Also of crucial importance is the shift in revenue from taxation to health insurance premiums, thereby reducing the burden of government. An irony of this new form of institutionalization is that it is not the children of the poor but young people from financially better-off homes who are most at risk. As Ira Schwartz has pointed out, curiously, racial minorities and other economically disadvantaged young people appear not to have these types of behavioural disorders and instead continue to be placed in criminal justice institutions. A disturbing feature of the new situation is the emerging symbiosis between private and public institutional provisions. The private mental health institutions, if they are to be attractive to parents who are adequately insured, must compare favourably with public institutions. Indeed, for the new private control system to flourish it may need, as is sometimes suggested by the advertising, a bad public counterpart.

Across the United States, a new institutional treatment apparatus is taking hold. The economic investment is so considerable that alternative approaches are rarely acknowledged. Out-patient work with young people and their families could be consistent with the developmental approach, but this is discouraged by the arrangements created by insurers and health care companies.

On television in the United States there has been a public service announcement which asks: 'It is ten o'clock ... Do you know where your children are?' This is a question not only for parents but for society as a whole.

Chapter Six

Getting Tough

Very little attention is paid to the basic elements of society, namely intermediate institutions; that is to say, small local groups in which face to face contact between the members is possible . . . the State must provide support to intermediate institutions and the control of conflict and of mediation must be left to them as much as possible. (Louk Hulsman, 1981, p. 155)

•

A developmental approach to youth crime poses tough and complex challenges to policy-makers and practitioners. Nothing less is required than a reversal of the existing policies which have become trapped within the approaches of punishment, welfare and treatment. Each of these three approaches serves to widen the nets of criminal justice, welfare and mental health, ultimately reinforcing incarcerative institutions, the very antithesis of normal growth and development. As a result increasing numbers of young people are becoming more deeply enmeshed in the apparatus of surveillance and incarceration. Reversal of these trends requires an insistence that the management of young people in trouble be entrusted to homes, schools and other developmental institutions.

The punishment approach to young people and crime once again dominates, just as it did during the first half of the nineteenth century. The predominance of punishment is in part due to support by liberals for the notions of just deserts and the deification of proportionality between harm done and dosage of pain; this alliance between old-fashioned punishers and liberal reformers is already showing signs of collapse. As the cruder consequences of the punishment approach become more obvious, it is probable that there will be a resurgence of interest in other approaches. The supporters of treatment and welfare wait hopefully in the wings, but both these approaches inevitably lead to the cul-de-sac of incarceration.

The claims of the welfare approach are more likely to be based on practice in Scotland than on the situation south of the border. In Scotland there has been an encouraging decline since 1973 in the number of young people up to the age of seventeen placed in incarcerative institutions. The factors responsible for this decline require close empirical exploration. It would be premature to put too much weight on the Scottish experience of the welfare approach. Furthermore, practice in Scotland may largely reflect the developmental ethos which underscored the Kilbrandon report of 1964.

It is the treatment approach which continues to demonstrate extraordinary resilience. Despite the damning research results on programme effectiveness and alarms raised as to the civil liberties of young people, it is treatment which seems most likely to challenge the punishment approach up to the turn of this century, just as it did at the close of the nineteenth century, when it was proposed that the penal reformatory at Elmira be regarded as a school or hospital. A hundred years later, the massive growth of incarceration within the mental health sector across the United States exceeded even the grandiose speculations of Zebulon Brockway.

It is misleading to regard the approaches of punishment and treatment as competitive. In fact, the two approaches enjoy a complementary relationship. From the treatment standpoint, the institutional setting reinforces the assumption that the problem is within the individual inmate. Treatment institutions attempt to be selective, accepting only inmates regarded as amenable. Punishment institutions are regarded as appropriate for non-amenable cases. Similarly, when treatment activities have a non-institutional basis, the focus is on young people regarded as amenable. Or, as put by Jerry Miller: 'A natural and understandable process of "creaming" takes place whereby the "most likely to succeed" are admitted to the program and kept inordinately long, thereby guaranteeing program peace and financial security' (Miller, 1978, p. 58). For the 'non-amenable', punishment institutions provide a suitable receptacle. Any perusal of social inquiry reports, prepared for courts by social workers and probation officers, confirms the widespread dumping of 'non-amenable' young people in punishment institutions. For example:

His response to supervision could be described as satisfactory but superficial, but it has not been successful in deterring him from breaking the law. It is perhaps unfortunate that at the point of leaving school and successfully obtaining work he should now face the real possibility of losing his liberty for the first time. However, despite the hardship this may cause, the court may feel that something needs to be done to try to break his pattern of offending and may consider a short period at detention centre as being the best method of doing this given that softer options have hitherto failed. (probation officer's report resulting in sentencing to a detention centre)

The trend towards a revitalized treatment approach is characterized by a new interest in physical technology. In particular, behaviour modification schemes lend themselves to the incarcerative institutions where the individual's environment can be controlled. Conveniently, these techniques also provide a means of institutional control. Medi-

165

cation, using a variety of drugs, is prevalent, especially in mental health settings. It also seems likely that direct medical interventions such as hormone implants and even surgery will be increasingly offered as ways of fixing the problem, and using the threat of punishment to gain the individual's consent.

The prospect of a revitalized treatment approach reinforcing the apparatus of punishment can only be regarded with alarm. Any retreat by liberals from punishment into treatment would further strengthen incarcerative institutions. An alternative route has to be charted. The book's central argument is that the developmental approach does suggest such a way forward. The traditional approaches threaten to move young people deeper into the official mechanisms of control; the developmental approach seeks to strengthen the commitment and capacity of home and school to hold on to young people.

Four fundamental steps must be taken to pursue seriously the developmental approach. In the first place, a reversal is required of existing financial incentives which favour incarceration. Instead, there must be powerful financial disincentives to shifting the action away from developmental institutions. The situation described by Lloyd Ohlin and his colleagues in the United States is germane to Britain:

The schools have been the subject of draconian cutbacks in a time when corrections have continued to develop. We are changing our society. We are retreating from working with youth in the school, and working more with them in corrections. If we do not change that pattern of shifting emphasis we will also no doubt shift the youth to where the emphasis is, and find ourselves working proportionately with more and more youth in corrections and fewer and fewer youth in the schools. (Miller and Ohlin, 1983, p. 237)

It is a paradox of the incarcerative institution that, despite the high financial costs incurred, it is offered as a 'no cost' solution to parents and teachers. The dramatic example of

seductive pressures on parents in Minnesota and other parts
of the United States demonstrates how medical insurance is
paving the way to psychiatric incarceration. In much the
same way, financial considerations may encourage teachers,
social workers and probation officers to rid themselves of
troublesome youngsters. When central government meets the
cost of incarceration in the prison system there is a disincen-
tive on local areas to set up alternatives. In 1983 the Home
Office attempted to dissuade eager detention centre staff from
blatant recruiting of inmates from the courts. In a memorandum to governors, the Home Office wrote: 'With reference
to enquiries about detention centre vacancies, we understand
from a number of justices' clerks that when courts telephone
to ask about the availability of places for people they propose
to sentence, it is not uncommon for them to be told not only
that there is a vacancy but also that the court is welcome to
send as many more offenders as it can find' (Home Office,
1983). Even in Massachusetts, where the state has abandoned
most of its incarcerative institutions, financial incentives exist
for regional offices to use 'no cost' secure beds.

The resurgence of private, including profit-making, activity
and funding presents yet a further obstacle to the path ahead.
Just as the private welfare institutions of the late nineteenth
century would ease cash flow problems by holding young
people for the maximum period, contemporary growth by
private interests poses problems of oversight and monitoring,
commonplace in the public process, but multiplied many
times in the private sector. The financial interests at stake are
enormous, and these will tend to gravitate to the incarcerative
institutions where the costs are highest. If there is to be
involvement by the private sector it must not be allowed to
have any sort of stake in incarcerative institutions. Commercial exploitation, as in some of the advertising by American
health care companies, of poorly endowed public incarceration should also be discouraged. Efforts by the private sector,

whether profit-making or otherwise, should be concentrated on supporting developmental institutions.

If the developmental approach is to be facilitated, the second fundamental step is to cut back on the use of incarcerative institutions before setting up new programmes in the community. The genius of Jerry Miller was his appreciation that decarceration had to begin at the 'deep end', with the most secure institution. The conventional strategy, as expressed in the Children and Young Persons Act 1969, is for institutions to be phased out as new alternatives become available. The result was that during the 1970s there was a fourfold increase in the number of young persons sent to the prison system, notwithstanding the rampant proliferation of Intermediate Treatment and other community-based initiatives. Had Jerry Miller been a rational bureaucrat the Lyman School for Boys would still be the oldest training school in the United States, operating alongside an array of new programmes. The overall net of criminal justice would have been widened because the new programmes would have almost certainly supplemented and not replaced incarceration.

The avoidance of net-widening requires that careful attention be given to how one set of decisions connects with decisions made elsewhere in the criminal process. If magistrates regard the caution as a first conviction, the result is inversion rather than diversion. The Woodlands Centre is one of the very few Intermediate Treatment programmes to take serious account of the gatekeeping role. The concerted effort to locate Woodlands near the deep end of criminal justice has had the consequence of making Basingstoke a custody-free zone. Elsewhere typical practice is to set up a programme and naïvely hope to reduce the use of prison system institutions. In January 1983 the government announced that £15 million would be made available over three years to support more intensive IT programmes designed specifically for those young people who would otherwise go to incarcerative institutions. But with little effort to monitor how the new initiatives fit into the local criminal justice process, much of this finance will do little other than divert social workers from more useful tasks.

The third step in moving to a developmental approach is to give close attention to linkages between criminal justice arrangements and developmental institutions. The real significance of Woodlands goes beyond changes effected in local criminal justice decision-making and extends to strengthening the capacity of the town to manage young people and crime. Although Woodlands is part of the criminal justice apparatus it has much in common with developmental institutions in that it seeks to hold on to young people by creating bonds for them with the locality. Acting, in part, as a substitute for home and school, the Woodlands strategy has a particular relevance to young people no longer at school and seeking independence from home.

Fourthly, it must be recognized that there may be self-serving resistance by professionals and others with a vested interest in existing arrangements to recognizing that the arena for action in dealing with young people and crime is mainly within the home and school. The campaign by the Magistrates' Association for short detention centre sentences and for direct sentencing powers to borstal/youth custody had a great deal to do with enhancing magistrates' autonomy over other professional groups within the court. In the early 1970s Scottish social workers successfully hijacked the Kilbrandon report from the education department. When Jerry Miller closed the training schools in Massachusetts it was the non-professionals and not the professional groups which came out in support. Professional social workers and others recognized the damaging consequences of the incarcerative institutions but remained uncertain where the dissolution left them. At one level it meant working with more difficult young people in the community without the threat of incarceration to gain compliance, but at another level it raised questions as to who might most appropriately work directly with young people.

If parents, teachers and other 'non-professionals' are to carry much more responsibility for holding on to young people in trouble, this will necessitate considerable adaptations by professionals. In particular there will need to be a shift from working directly with young people to providing support to developmental institutions. These support services require different levels of skill which, in turn, have implications for professional training.

Far from amounting to a soft option, the developmental approach poses many tough challenges to policy and practice, as is indicated by the following specific proposals.

1. Broad-Ranging Policies to Strengthen the Home

Covered under this heading are a variety of policies encompassing housing, health and social services. The common goal is to ease pressures on the parental task of bringing up children. In part these pressures are economic, and child benefit allowances, housing subsidies and day care form key parts of the package. But, as the Minnesota saga demonstrates, the need goes beyond economics. Stresses and strains within the home cut across all social and economic groups. It is tough work holding on to young people in trouble, regardless of social circumstances. Support required for the home can vary from what a relative or friend might provide to specialized family counselling. There can be no justification for adding to parental pressures. For example, fining parents for their children's misdeeds, as allowed for by the Criminal

Justice Act 1982, is directly counter to the developmental approach.

2. Emphasis on the School's Pastoral Role

There has to be a massive injection of resources into schools and other educational institutions, especially with respect to the strengthening of pastoral responsibilities. This involves broadening basic teacher training and in-service training, and provision of a variety of specialists whose task is to support teachers and, when necessary, to work directly with pupils. The 20 per cent drop in the numbers of young people of school age during the 1980s provides an opportune breathing space for schools to reallocate resources so as to be better able to hold on to troublesome pupils. As the Lushington and Kilbrandon reports had done before, the Black report regarded the school as being involved with the development of the whole child, leading it to recommend 'a school-based forum in which the appropriate counsellor, the education welfare officer, the educational psychologist and the social worker familiar with the catchment area of the school might combine [so as to bring about] . . . the early identification and resolution of the problems facing children and young people and the construction of an integrated programme of help for children in need from the pre-school age' (Black, 1979, pp. 9–10).

3. Support Arrangements beyond School

There needs to be urgent exploration of additional supports that might see young adults through difficult phases. This is especially important where the role of the home and school is diminished and where employment prospects may be non-existent. Gaps in the provision of developmental institutions for this older age group cry out for creative practice. One of the most valuable resources that may be harnessed in this effort is the potential for mutual support among young adults.

The remaining proposals for policy more directly address criminal justice and refer to the situation pertaining in England and Wales. The common theme is to keep young people out of the criminal justice process so as to be consistent with the basic purpose of strengthening developmental institutions.

4. The Age of Criminal Responsibility

Only about one in eight of ten- and eleven-year-olds, where prosecution was possible, were taken to court in 1983. Setting the age of criminal responsibility at twelve confirms progressive police practice.

5. Avoiding Criminal Law

Informal cautioning by the police should be encouraged so as to reverse the trend whereby formal cautioning has replaced informal cautioning. The crown prosecutor should be encouraged to filter further cases away from the court. Formal cautions by either police or prosecutor should not be cited in any subsequent court case. An important feature of the proposal is to increase significantly the level of formal cautioning of young persons aged seventeen and over. In 1983, of all seventeen-year-olds who were found guilty or cautioned only 6 per cent were cautioned, compared with 32 per cent of sixteen-year-olds.

6. Jurisdiction of the Juvenile Court

Under this proposal the juvenile court would have jurisdiction over 12–17 year olds. Setting the maximum age at seventeen is consistent with the age of legal majority (as well as being the peak age for many types of offences). This proposal would have the effect of keeping seventeen-year-olds out of the prison system. In 1983, 5,500 seventeen-year-olds were received on sentence by the prison system.

The juvenile court would deal only with persons charged with criminal offences, with the courts' civil responsibilities handled by a new family court. The juvenile court would have the following main features:

- The juvenile bench would reside in the petty sessional division.
- The recruitment of magistrates would closely reflect the socio-economic and ethnic features of the petty sessional division.
- Magistrates would be expected to complete a rigorous training course during the first year of their appointment and attend subsequent on-going training sessions.
- Juvenile court magistrates would be recruited in their twenties and thirties and their appointment would not be extended beyond the age of fifty.

Juvenile court proceedings would share the legal safeguards available in the adult court. The more informal traditions of the juvenile court would be retained so as to ensure that the young persons and their parents fully understand the proceedings and their rights.

7. Powers of the Juvenile Court

Incarcerative institutions would only be available at the local level of government and, except for grave offences, the maximum duration of such sentences would be nine months. This proposal outlaws the use of the prison system for this age group (remand would also be restricted to the local level), as was envisaged by the Children and Young Persons Act 1969 that was, however, repealed in 1982. The number of incarcerative beds would be limited by central government, which would also be responsible for standard-setting and inspection.

Care orders would not be available to the juvenile court. The basis for court-ordered non-incarcerative initiatives would be the supervision order. This proposal places the supervision order in a pivotal position and is intended to encourage local agencies to establish a network of programmes. The purposes of such programmes would include support and guidance of the young person together with opportunities for reparation and compensation. The essence of supervision is that it consists of an umbrella of activities in which young people might be involved during their developmental years. It is important to stress that supervision is not simply one point on a tariff scale but encompasses a variety of options, each of which may need to be used for any one young person. The proposal builds upon attempts to consolidate the supervision order and emphasizes its prominent position so that a variety of dynamic and flexible responses to youth crime are prompted at the local level.

8. Reduced Tariff for 18–20 Year Olds

Young adults would be tried in the criminal courts but would be subject to sentencing guidelines to be set by a sentencing commission providing a reduced tariff compared with older adults. The intention would be to stem the increasing flow of young adults into the prison system on remand and on sentence. To complement the initiatives of the sentencing commission, new fiscal mechanisms would be required to encourage probation departments and other agencies to extend programmes and support services for this age group.

9. Effective Oversight of all Types of Incarcerative Institutions

Central government must effectively monitor the use of all forms of incarceration, public and private. As a minimum there should be 'a statistical watch on all types of asylum, by whoever's ownership they flourish, and by whatever name they pass' (Guttridge and Warren, 1984, p. 24).

The overriding need is for public policy to take full account of good existing practice. In other words, there has to be recognition by policy-makers that the most effective and least damaging work with young people in trouble occurs outside formal and specialized arrangements. It is informal and often intuitive action within the home and school that provides the best response to these young people. It is developmental institutions which quietly demonstrate that, above all else, what is needed is time.

References

Abbott, Jack Henry (1982), *In the Belly of the Beast*, New York, Village Books.

Austin, James, and Krisberg, Barry (1982), 'The unmet promise of alternatives to incarceration', *Crime and Delinquency*, pp. 374–409.

Ball, Caroline (1983), 'Secret justice: The use made of school reports in the juvenile court', *British J. Social Work*, pp. 197–205.

Bennett, Trevor (1979), 'The social distribution of criminal labels', *British Journal of Criminology, 19*, pp. 134–145.

Berlins, Marcel, and Wansell, Geoffrey (1974), *Caught in the Act: Children, Society and the Law*, Harmondsworth, Penguin.

Black Report (1979), *Report of the Children and Young Persons Review Group*, Chairman, Sir Harold Black, Belfast, HMSO.

Brim, Orville G., and Kagan, Jerome (eds.) (1980), *Constancy and Change in Human Development*, Cambridge, Mass., Harvard University Press.

Bruce, Nigel (1982), 'Historical background', *The Scottish Juvenile Justice System* (eds. F. M. Martin and K. Murray), Edinburgh, Scottish Academic Press.

Cadogan Report (1938), *Report of the Departmental Committee on Corporal Punishment*, Chairman, Sir Edward Cadogan, Cmnd. 568, London, HMSO.

Carlebach, Julius (1970), *Caring for Children in Trouble*, London, Routledge and Kegan Paul.

Carpenter, Mary (1851), *Reformatory Schools, for the Children of the Perishing and Dangerous Classes and for Juvenile Offenders*, London, Gilpin.

Castle, Barbara (1980), *The Castle Diaries, 1974–1976*, London, Weidenfeld and Nicolson.

Cawson, Pat and Martell, Mary (1979), *Children Referred to Closed Units*, London, DHSS Research Report No. 5.

Christie, Nils (1982), *Limits to Pain*, Oxford, Martin Robertson.

Citizens' League of Minnesota (1984), *Meeting the Crisis in Institutional Care*, Minneapolis.

Cline, Hugh F. (1980), 'Criminal behaviour over the life span', *Constancy and Change in Human Development* (eds. O. G. Brim and J. Kagan), Cambridge, Mass., Harvard, pp. 641–74.

Coates, R., Miller, A. D., and Ohlin, L. E. (1973), 'Strategic innovation in the process of deinstitutionalization: The University of Massachusetts conference', *Closing Correctional Institutions* (ed. Y. Bakal), Lexington, Mass., Lexington Books.

Coates, R. B., and Miller, A. D. (1975), 'Evaluating large scale social service systems in changing environments: The case of correctional agencies', *Journal of Research in Crime and Delinquency*, 12, pp. 92–106.

Coleman, James, et al. (1974), *Youth: Transition to Adulthood*, Chicago, University of Chicago Press.

Dillon, Carol, et al. (1982), 'In re Roger S.: The impact of a child's due process victory on the California mental health system', *California Law Review*, 70, pp. 373–478.

Driscoll, Judge Margaret (1977), *Juvenile Justice Digest*, Vol. 7, 5 April.

Edwards, S. (1976), *Treatment in Security*, London, Institute for the Study and Treatment of Delinquency.

Empey, LaMar (1976), a monograph.

Expenditure Committee of the House of Commons (1975), *Eleventh Report, The Children and Young Persons Act 1969*, 2 vols.

Farrington, David (1977), 'The effects of public labelling', *British Journal of Criminology*, 17, pp. 112–25.

Farrington, David (1981), 'Delinquency from 10 to 25', unpublished paper.

Farrington, David, and Bennett, Trevor (1981), 'Police cautioning of juveniles in London', *British Journal of Criminology*, 21, pp. 123–35.

Fox, Sanford (1974), 'Juvenile justice reform: The child's right to punishment', *Juvenile Justice*, 25, pp. 2–6.

Giller, Henri (1982), unpublished paper for NACRO.

Gladstone Report (1895), *Report of the Departmental Committee on Prisons*, Chairman, Herbert Gladstone, C. 7702.

References

Green, Chris (1983*a*), 'The Woodlands Centre: A fresh approach to the management of delinquency', unpublished paper.

Green, Chris (1983*b*), 'The Woodlands I.T. Centre: A community response to delinquency', unpublished paper.

Greenberg, David (1983), 'Age and crime', *Encyclopedia of Crime and Justice* (ed. S. H. Kadish), New York Free Press.

Guttridge, Patricia, and Warren, Carol (1984), 'Adolescent psychiatric hospitalization and social control', unpublished paper.

Harshbarger Report (1977), *The Issue of Security in a Community-Based System of Juvenile Justice*, Chairman, Scott Harshbarger, Boston, Department of Youth Services.

Hazel, Nancy (1978), 'The use of family placements in the treatment of delinquency', *Alternative Strategies for Coping With Crime* (ed. N. Tutt), Oxford, Blackwell, pp. 82–102.

Home Office (1959), *Penal Practice in a Changing Society: Aspects of Future Development*, Cmnd. 645.

Home Office (1965), *The Child, The Family and the Young Offender*, Cmnd. 2742.

Home Office (1968), *Children in Trouble*, Cmnd. 3601.

Home Office (1980), *Young Offenders*, Cmnd. 8045.

Home Office, (1983), *Criminal Justice Act 1982: Advice to Courts on Sentencing*, Memorandum from Prison Department to detention centre wardens, 20 May 1983.

Home Office (1984*a*), *Tougher Regimes in Detention Centres*, Prison Department Young Offender Psychology Unit, London, Home Office.

Home Office (1984*b*), *Cautioning by the Police: A Consultative Document*, London, Home Office.

Hood, Roger (1965), *Borstal Re-assessed*, London, Heinemann.

Hulsman, Louk (1981), 'Penal reform in the Netherlands – Bringing the criminal justice system under control', *Howard Journal*, pp. 150–59.

Ingleby Report (1960), *Report of the Committee on Children and Young Persons*, Chairman, Lord Ingleby, Cmnd. 1191.

Irwin, John (1970), *The Felon*, Englewood Cliffs, N J, Prentice-Hall.

Jay Report (1977), *Children and Young Persons in Custody*, Report of a NACRO Working Party, Chairman, Peter Jay, London, NACRO.

Junger-Tas, Josine, 'The juvenile justice system in Holland', unpublished paper.

Kagan, Jerome (1979), *The Growth of the Child: Reflections on Human Development*, Hassocks, Sussex, Harvester Press.

Keane, Barry (1972), 'The Teeside after-care group', unpublished paper.

Kilbrandon Report (1964), *Children and Young Persons: Scotland*, Chairman, Lord Kilbrandon, Cmnd. 2306.

Kilbrandon, Lord (1976), Introduction to *Children's Hearings* (eds. F. Martin and K. Murray), Edinburgh, Scottish Academic Press.

Krisberg, Barry, and Schwartz, Ira (1983), 'Rethinking juvenile justice', *Crime and Delinquency*, 29, pp. 333–64.

Landau, Simba, and Nathan, Gad (1983), 'Selecting delinquents for cautioning in the London Metropolitan Area', *British Journal of Criminology*, 23, pp. 128–49.

Laugharne, Albert (1983), unpublished paper to NACRO.

Laycock, Gloria, and Tarling, Roger (1984), in Home Office Consultative Document on Police Cautioning, Home Office, pp. 36–47.

Lerman, Paul (1975), *Community Treatment and Social Control*, Chicago, University of Chicago Press.

Lerman, Paul (1982), *Deinstitutionalization and the Welfare State*, New Brunswick, NJ, Rutgers University Press.

Lushington Report (1896), *Report of Departmental Committee on Reformatory and Industrial Schools*, Chairman, Sir Godfrey Lushington.

McGillis, Daniel, and Spangenberg, Robert (1976), *The Camp Hill Project: An Assessment*, report prepared for the National Institute for Juvenile Justice and Delinquency Prevention, US Department of Justice by Abt Associates.

Maher, Peter (1984), 'The frontiers of teacher responsibility', paper to Howard League.

Malony Report (1927), *Report of Departmental Committee on the Treatment of Young Offenders*, Chairman, Sir Thomas Malony, Cmnd. 2831.

Manton, Jo (1976), *Mary Carpenter and the Children of the Streets*, London, Heinemann Educational Books.

Massachusetts Advocacy Center (1980), *Delinquent Justice – Juvenile Detention Practice in Massachusetts*, Boston.

References

Massachusetts Department of Youth Services (1982), *Classification Policy Guidelines Concerning Entrance into Secure Treatment Facilities*, Boston.

Miller, A. D., and Ohlin, L. E. (1983), *Final Report of Research on Correctional Reforms in the Massachusetts Department of Youth Services*, Harvard Law School, mimeo.

Miller, Jerome (1973), *Closing Correctional Institutions* (ed. Y. Bakal), Lexington, Mass., Lexington Books, pp. 3–12.

Miller, Jerome (1978), 'Systems of control and the serious juvenile offender', *The Serious Juvenile Offender*, Washington DC Dept of Justice.

Millham, Spencer, et al. (1978), *Locking Up Children*, Farnborough, Gower.

Monck, Elizabeth (1983), 'Expulsion and supervision', *Contact* (ILEA newsletter), 9 September.

Murphy, Edward (1984), 'Deinstitutionalization: Myth and reality', unpublished paper, August 1984.

NACRO (1984), *School Reports in the Juvenile Court*, London, NACRO.

Note (1978), 'The mental hospitalization of children and the limits of parental autonomy', *Yale Law Review*, 88, pp. 186–216.

Owen, Pauline (1984), unpublished paper on the Woodlands Centre.

Parker, Howard (1974), *View from the Boys*, Newton Abbot, David and Charles.

Pask, Roger (1982), 'Court reports', paper prepared for NACRO.

Pisciotta, Alexander (1983), 'Scientific reform: The new "penology" at Elmira, 1876–1900', *Crime and Delinquency*, (October), pp. 613–30.

Power, M. J., et al. (1967), 'Delinquent schools', *New Society*, 10, pp. 542–3.

Power, M. J., et al. (1972), 'Neighbourhood, school and juveniles before the courts', *British Journal of Criminology*, 12, pp. 111–32.

Radzinowicz, Leon (1952), *Detention in remand homes*, London, MacMillan.

Reynolds, David and Sullivan, Michael (1981), 'The effects of school: A radical faith restated', *Problem behaviour in the Secondary School* (ed. B. Graham), London, Croom Helm.

Riley, David, and Shaw, Margaret (1985), *Parental Supervision and*

Juvenile Delinquency, Home Office Research Unit Study no. 83, London, HMSO.

Rose, Stephen M. (1979), 'Deciphering deinstitutionalization: Complexities in policy and program analysis', *Milbank Memorial Fund Quarterly*, 57, pp. 429–60.

Ruck, S. K. (ed.) (1951), *Paterson on Prisons*, London, Frederick Muller.

Rutherford, Andrew (1973), 'Workshops: Linking the institution and urban area', *Prison Service Journal*, 14, pp. 1–6.

Rutherford, Andrew (1977), *Youth Crime Policy in the United States*, London, Institute for the Study and Treatment of Delinquency.

Rutter, Michael, et al. (1979), *Fifteen Thousand Hours: Secondary Schools and Their Effects on Children*, London, Open Books.

Rutter, Michael, and Giller, Henri (1983), *Juvenile Delinquency: Trends and Prospectives*, Harmondsworth, Penguin.

Sarnecki, Jerzy (1983), 'Research into juvenile crime in Sweden', *Information Bulletin of the National Swedish Council for Crime Prevention*, Stockholm.

Schur, Edwin (1973), *Radical Non-Intervention*, Englewood Cliffs, NJ, Prentice-Hall.

Schwartz, Ira, Jackson-Beeck, Marilyn, and Anderson, Roger (1984), 'The "Hidden" system of juvenile control', *Crime and Delinquency*, 30, pp. 371–85.

Select Committee on Social Services (1984), *Children in Care*, Session 83/84, HC 360–61.

Sparks, Richard F., and Hood, Roger (1968), Introduction to *The Residential Treatment of Disturbed and Delinquent Boys*, Cambridge, Institute of Criminology, pp. 7–11.

Steer, David (1970), *Police Cautions – A Study in the Exercise of Police Discretion*, Oxford University Penal Research Unit, Oxford, Blackwell.

Tempkin J. (1973), 'The child, the family and the young offender – Swedish style', *Modern Law Review*, 36, pp. 569–86.

Templewood, Lord (1954), *Nine Troubled Years*, London, Collins.

Troup, Sir Edward (1925), *The Home Office*, London, G. P. Putnam.

Tutt, Norman (1984), 'Civil liberties and youth', *Civil Liberties 1984* (ed. P. Waddington), Oxford, Martin Robertson, pp. 289–308.

Warren, Carol (1981), 'New forms of social control: The myth of deinstitutionalization', *American Behavioral Scientist*, 24, pp. 724–40.

References

Warren, Carol (1984), 'Privatizing the public sector: Health care and "social control" institutions', *New Management*, 1, pp. 29–33.

Watson, John (1942), *The Child and the Magistrates' Court*, London, Cape.

West, Donald (1982), *Delinquency: Its Roots, Careers and Prospects*, London, Heinemann.

Whiffin, Alan K. (1972), 'Group work: An experiment in Borstal through care', unpublished paper.

Wilson, Harriett (1980), 'Parental supervision, a neglected aspect of delinquency', *British Journal of Criminology*, 20, pp. 203–5.

Wolfgang, Marvin, et al. (1972), *Delinquency in a Birth Cohort*, Chicago, University of Chicago Press.

Younger Report (1974), *Young Adult Offenders*, Report of the Advisory Council on the Penal System, Chairman, Sir Kenneth Younger, London, HMSO.

Zimring, Franklin (1978), *Confronting Youth Crime*, New York, Holmes and Meier.

Index

Index

Index

Regnery, A., 99
Remand, 91–2
Remand centres, 46, 49, 52
Remand homes, 43, 48
Residential care, 16–7, 20
Reynolds, D., 117–19
Riley, D., 116
Rose, G., 52
Rose, S. M., 150
Roslingdale Detention Center, Massachusetts, 89–90
Royal College of Psychiatrists, 20
Royal Commission on Reformatories and Approved Schools (1883), 32
Ruggles-Brise, E., 38
Rutherford, A., 99, 132
Rutter, M., 117–19, 126

Sargent, F., 68, 73–4
Sargent, J., 73–4
Sarnecki, J., 110
Schools
  court reports by, 123–6
  in London, 117–19, 120–21
  in South Wales, 119–20
  offences in, 122–3
  role of, 117–21, 126–7, 171
  special units in, 121
  suspensions from, 120, 121
Schur, E., 14
Schwartz, I., 92, 99, 105, 148–50, 159–61
Scotland, 55, 164
  see also: Kilbrandon report
Secure beds, 78, 83–92, 167
Select Committee on Social Services (1984), 16–17, 20
Shaw, M., 116

Shirley industrial school, Massachusetts, 69, 75
'Short sharp punishment', 51–2, 65–6
Sims, R., 64
Society for Reformation of Prison Discipline, 49
South Wales, research on schools in, 117–19
Spangenberg, R., 106
Sparks, R. F., 58
Status offenders, 105
  see also: CHINS
Steer, D., 131
Stranger, R. C., 59, 61
Sullivan, M., 119
Supervision order, 56, 174
Sweden
  affluence criminality, 110
  role of family in, 116

Tarling, R., 131
Task force on juvenile crime (Massachusetts, 1981), 81, 94
Tempkin, J., 116
Toby, J., 23
Training schools, 26, 68, 69, 75–6, 105
Transportation, 27–9
Troup, Sir E., 44
Truancy, 117, 120
Turner, S., 29, 32
Tutt, N., 129

Unemployment, effect of, 128
Unified Delinquency Intervention Services (UDIS), 106
Utah, 105

Waller, Sir M., 45
Wansell, G., 61

MORE ABOUT PENGUINS, PELICANS, PEREGRINES AND PUFFINS

For further information about books available from Penguins please write to Dept EP, Penguin Books Ltd, Harmondsworth, Middlesex UB7 ODA.

In the U.S.A.: For a complete list of books available from Penguins in the United States write to Dept DG, Penguin Books, 299 Murray Hill Parkway, East Rutherford, New Jersey 07073.

In Canada: For a complete list of books available from Penguins in Canada write to Penguin Books Canada Ltd, 2801 John Street, Markham, Ontario L3R 1B4.

In Australia: For a complete list of books available from Penguins in Australia write to the Marketing Department, Penguin Books Australia Ltd, P.O. Box 257, Ringwood, Victoria 3134.

In New Zealand: For a complete list of books available from Penguins in New Zealand write to the Marketing Department, Penguin Books (N.Z.) Ltd, Private Bag, Takapuna, Auckland 9.

In India: For a complete list of books available from Penguins in India write to Penguin Overseas Ltd, 706 Eros Apartments, 56 Nehru Place, New Delhi 110019.